Shadows of the Messiah in the Torah
Volume One
Revised Edition

And beginning with Moses and all the prophets, He explained what was said in all the scriptures concerning Himself.
Luke 24:27

Hebrew Roots Teachings for Home Studies
by
Dan and Brenda Cathcart

Cover Design: Dan Cathcart

A Note From the authors:

With a great love for God's word and a desire to see the Hebraic nature of the scripters taught to the Nations, this volume has been compiled from studies conducted in our home over the last several years. It is our sincere prayer that this study volume will enrich your life and those who attend your home study or small group. May the LORD bless you and your family.

Dan & Brenda Cathcart

Published by Moed Publishing, Auburn, WA

Visit us on the web at www.moedministries.com

Table of Contents

Preface: Starting a Home Bible Study

We've been Christians for all of our adult lives and considered ourselves knowledgeable about the scriptures, but as we have rediscovered the basic Hebraic nature of the scriptures, we have discovered that we knew almost nothing. We are just beginning to really learn about the character of God and His incredible mercy in that He planned our redemption from the very beginning of creation. As we learn more and more about who God is, we have become closer to Him and know what an incredible gift His salvation is. Now, we don't have to tell ourselves we should witness or behave in a certain way, it all just comes bubbling out. We can't help but share about God and the redemption He offers through His son, Yeshua (Jesus). And so, we want to share some of what we have learned.

We've chosen to focus these studies on finding the Messiah in the Tanakh, that is, the Old Testament. Our inspiration is Yeshua's words when He spoke to two of His followers on the road to Emmaus after His resurrection. Our theme verse is Luke 24:27, **"And beginning with Moses and all the prophets, He explained to them what was said in all the scriptures concerning Himself."**(NIV) What did Yeshua teach them? What scriptures was He referring to? The only scriptures in existence at that time were those of the Tanakh. And so, we chose the topic of "Shadows of Messiah" to search out those very scriptures that Yeshua referred to. Imagine our surprise to find that almost everything in the Tanakh points to Yeshua haMashiach, Yeshua our Messiah!

When we begin to see how often and with such incredible detail that God reveals His redemption plan and Yeshua the Messiah, there is no mistaking Him for any other. As Messiah, He must be uniquely qualified; He must be a part of God Himself. No other can bring about the redemption of mankind. We can know without doubt that, in the words of Paul (Shaul) in Ephesians 2:8-9, "by faith you have been saved by grace, not of works lest any man should boast."

As we approach the Day of the LORD, when Yeshua comes again, it is more and more important that we be able to recognize Him when He comes. Yeshua Himself said that in the latter days false christs and prophets would appear deceiving the very elect if that were possible.

> Mk 13:22 For false Christs and false prophets will appear and perform signs and miracles to deceive the elect-- if that were possible. (NIV)

This is so true. Even now, churches are preaching Yeshua as a "good man" we can model ourselves after; that good works is all that God requires. Others teach that the god of the Muslims is the same as the God of the Bible. Those who are grounded in scripture know how very wrong that is. It is completely contrary to the God and the Messiah revealed in the scriptures. Come and rediscover the Hebrew roots of your faith. You will never be the same.

Rediscovering our Hebrew roots is why we deliberately use some Hebrew terms. Most of the Bible was originally written in Hebrew. The whole Hebrew way of thinking, their mindset, is different from the Western way of thinking which is based on ancient Greek philosophy. The words in Hebrew take on the cultural meaning of the words, and by their use, we enter into that way of thinking. For example, the very name of Jesus is really Yeshua which means "He saves" or "salvation." When we read the words of Psalm 118:14, "The Lord is my strength and song, and is become my salvation (KJV)," we realize that this verse is talking about "my Yeshua." God has literally become "my Yeshua." Salvation only comes through "my Yeshua."

We started our home Bible study after attending a newly found, Hebrew roots teaching church for about 6 months. We were so excited we just had to start a Bible study! We meet twice a month on the first and third Friday. Since the Biblical Sabbath begins on Friday evening, we decided to combine the Bible study with a meal to kick off the Sabbath. So, we have a potluck to start the evening followed by the Bible study.

The materials have all been developed from topics brought up during the weekly Sabbath teachings or from the weekly Torah Club Bible study that he teaches. Sometimes, we will get a short snippet of information that intrigues us and that will lead to a study. At home, we get out our Sabbath notes, our Torah Club notes, Strong's Concordance and several translations of the Bible and then dig in. A good Study Bible that helps to link verses is a must! We use several as well as many on-line resources..

The best way to start a Home Bible study is to jump in and start!

1. Choose a day and time. It can be weekly, monthly or bi-monthly. You won't be able to please everyone so just choose what works best for you. Allow about an hour and a half for the study portion of each meeting. You should be able to complete the study materials in about an hour depending on the group. Extra time is good for questions, discussion and just getting to know each other.

2. Invite friends, neighbors, family members. You might encourage them to bring a friend also. The materials included in this book are not sequential so new people can start any time. Be enthusiastic and positive. Let your excitement show; it's contagious!

3. Leaders should read through all the material before teaching. It is especially helpful for the leader to be familiar with the contexts of the scriptures, so take some time and look up the scriptures and read the broader context of the passages the scriptures are taken from.

4. Pray! It's amazing how God opens our eyes and ears to see and understand when we ask Him. Pray before preparing and pray before teaching.

How to use these materials:

1. Each lesson contains two parts. One part is a detailed guide for the use of the leader. We have found it easier to teach if all the scriptures are written out in the notes so we've written out all the scriptures. The second part consists of note pages for students along with questions to facilitate group discussion and comment. Make copies of the student notes and questions for each participant. To facilitate making copies of the student notes and other handouts easier, these items are available in PDF format from our web site at no additional charge. Go to MoedMinistries.com/bookstore.html for details of how to download the free PDFs.

2. There are general handouts materials located at the end of this book for all study participants. These are also available as PDF files. The Hebrew Alphabet Chart should be available for all the sessions since most lessons have references to the Hebrew language or alphabet. The glossary is also useful especially for participants who drop in occasionally for a lesson.

3. The original Hebrew was written in pictographs. Each letter comes from a picture and retains the meaning of the picture. Many words make compelling "word pictures." Those are included in a separate text block. They may be used where they are inserted in the page or at the beginning or end of the lesson. Having handouts of the Hebrew Alphabet Chart available at all the studies is helpful for the students to refer to whenever a word picture is presented.

4. The first lesson, "Searching God's Word," is relatively short and introduces word pictures and Hebrew language concepts and study methods that will be used throughout the material. It is a good first study leaving time to perform introductions and discuss the format of the studies.

5. Most of the lessons contain references to the original Hebrew or Greek. The number associated with the word is its reference in the Strong's Concordance and Dictionary.

Preface to the Second Edition

Over three years have gone by since we started our Bible study focusing on finding the Shadows of Messiah in the Torah. We have learned much in our journey and as we revisited this first volume of Shadows of Messiah, we found we needed to make some revisions that reflect our growth as students of the Word and our experience in writing.

The first thing we have done is to add some consistency in length to the studies. We've added more material and depth to the shorter studies, God Dwells with Man, To Your Seed, and the Woman Caught in Adultery. For the study the Hem of the Garment, we added an appendix on how to tie the tzit-tzit. As our understanding of scripture has grown, we've gone back and refined the lessons In the Time of Noah, The Kingdom of Heaven Suffers Violence, and Isaac's Marriage and the Bride of Christ. We've made other minor changes in some of the other studies. While we continue to want the scriptures to be the main focus and not our own words, we were a bit terse with our words so we've added a few words to try to nail down the points.

The most significant change is the addition of discussion questions at the end of each lesson. This allows for more diversity in presenting the material and promotes more interaction with the material and between the participants. We didn't want the questions to just rehash the material in the lessons, so we've tried to pose questions that lead to deeper thinking and putting that understanding into words. We've included questions that extend beyond the lesson itself. Some questions connect the lessons together. Other questions ask the participant to apply concepts to their own lives. We have also added an appendix listing some additional resources. Finally, we've used the name Yeshua instead of Jesus reflecting His identity as a Jewish man of His day observing all the commandments of the Torah. This also reflects that He is the Jewish Messiah God promised to Abraham, Isaac, Jacob and the children of Israel. As Paul tells us in Romans Yeshua came first to the Jew and then to the Gentile; we are grafted into the commonwealth of Israel, not Israel into the Gentiles.

The Student notes, discussion questions and other general handout materials in PDF format are available for FREE download on our website at MoedMinistries.com/bookstore.html.

Our sincere prayer is that these materials serve to draw you nearer to God, that you have a firmer foundation of what and who you believe in. As the turmoil of these days increases and conflicting messages about the identity of the God of Abraham, Isaac, Jacob and Yeshua proliferate, we hope that you will "…hold firmly till the end the confidence we had at first." (Heb. 3:14)

Shalom and be blessed,
Dan and Brenda Cathcart,
Moed Ministries International

8

Searching God's Word

When we read and study the Bible in our English translations, we can and often do miss some key ingredients to a deeper understanding and richness of God's word. Most of the Bible was originally written in the Hebrew language and is from an ancient culture and people. Although the style of writing has changed over the centuries, the content, complete with unusual anomalies, has remained unchanged since the time Moses wrote the first five books of the Bible in the ancient form of Hebrew. For nearly four thousand years, generation after generation of scribes and priests have carefully preserved God's words to Moses and the Children of Israel. Each Torah scroll is meticulously copied and thoroughly checked for any deviations before it is certified as an authentic Torah scroll. God the Father has revealed to us through these same scriptures His plan for our redemption and given us insight into His very nature.

It says in Proverbs 25:2 "It is the glory of God to conceal a matter, but the glory of kings to search it out." (KJV) But how are we to study and discover the things which he has "concealed" in Hebrew when our Bibles are in English? It would make sense to take a serious look at it original language in which it was written as well as the original cultural and historical context. This may at first seem an insurmountable task for the average person, but it will prove not to be as daunting as it might first appear. We take it one small bite at a time. And as we discover the hidden treasures of the Word of God in the original Hebrew language, we will find ourselves eager to search for more and more!

We are commanded to study God's word as the Apostle Paul told Timothy.

> 2Tim 2:15 Be diligent to present yourself approved to God, a worker who does not need to be ashamed, rightly dividing the word of truth. (NKJV)

Later Paul reminds Timothy that:

> 2 Tim 3:16 All Scripture is given by inspiration of God, and is profitable for doctrine, for reproof, for correction, for instruction in righteousness, 17 that the man of God may be complete, thoroughly equipped for every good work. (NKJV)

The only scripture that Paul and the rest of the first century apostles had was what we know today as the "Old Testament." This is what the Jewish people refer to as the Tanakh which consists of the Torah, the Prophets and the Writings. It is in these scriptures that Paul found the Gospel of Yeshua. Woven throughout the Torah, Prophets and writings are the shadows of the Messiah. These are the scriptures that Paul and the other apostles of Yeshua used throughout their ministries to carry the "Mystery of the Gospel" to the Jews first and then to the Gentiles of their time. As we study these same scriptures, viewing them from the same perspective as the early apostles did, we too will discover the same Gospel message that they preached in the first century.

A. What is the Torah? We think of it as the "Jewish Scriptures." The first 5 books of the Old Testament are the Torah. But there are references in the New Testament scriptures that Yeshua and the apostles referred to the entire body of scripture as the Torah.

> 1 Co 14:21 In the law it is written: "With men of other tongues and other lips I will speak to this people; And yet, for all that, they will not hear Me," says the Lord. (NKJV)

In this Epistle, Paul quotes the Prophet Isaiah (28:11-12) saying "In the law it is written" The word "Law" (Greek nomos) is used throughout the New Testament scriptures in reference to the Torah. Here and elsewhere, Paul refers to all of scripture as Torah (law or nomos).

#8451. תורה towrah, to-raw' or torah {to-raw'}; from 3384; a precept or statute, especially the Decalogue or Pentateuch:--law.

#3384. ירה yarah, yaw-raw', yara; {yaw-raw'}; a primitive root; properly, to flow as water (i.e. to rain); transitively, to lay or throw (especially an arrow, i.e. to shoot); figuratively, to point out (as if by aiming the finger), to teach:--(+) archer, cast, direct, inform, instruct, lay, shew, shoot, teach(-er,-ing), through.

We can see that the Torah is much more than just rules and regulations. The Torah contains God's teachings and instructions on how to live; on how to approach a holy God. It points out examples of men and women of faith and righteousness—these two always go together—as well as examples of rebellion and apostasy. It reveals the sinful nature of man and the righteous requirements of God. It reveals God's incredible mercy showing us our need for a redeemer and how God Himself will meet that need.

There is an interesting connection between the words Torah and sin. Sin is the Hebrew word chattah.

#2403. חטאה chatta'ah, khat-taw-aw' from 2398; an offence (sometimes habitual sinfulness), and its penalty, occasion, sacrifice, or expiation; also (concretely) an offender:--punishment (of sin), purifying(-fication for sin), sin(-ner, offering).

#2398. חטא chata', khaw-taw' a primitive root; properly, **to miss**; hence (figuratively and generally) to sin; by inference, to forfeit, lack, expiate, repent, (causatively) lead astray, condemn:--bear the blame, cleanse, commit (sin), by fault, harm he hath done, loss, miss, (make) offend(-er), offer for sin, purge, purify (self), make reconciliation.

Torah comes from a word meaning to point out, to shoot an arrow; that is to hit the mark. Sin comes from a word meaning to miss; that is miss the mark! In the Hebrew manner of thought, they are opposites of each other.

Hebrew word picture: Hebrew is read right to left
Torah: תורה
Tav: ת Cross, covenant or sign of the covenant
Vav: ו Nail, tent peg, to secure
Resh: ר Person especially the highest person, head
Hey: ה Reveal. At the end of a word hey can mean what comes from or out of, belonging to

Torah: The covenant secured by the highest person revealed or that which comes from the highest person nailed to the cross.

The Hebrew word picture for Torah shows us that the Torah is the covenant that Yeshua secures by His death. The apostle John defines sin as disobedience of Torah.

1 Joh 3:4 Everyone who sins breaks the law; in fact, sin is lawlessness. (NIV)

B. The study of the Torah is one of the commandments of the Torah.

De 6:7 "You shall teach them diligently to your children, and shall talk of them when you sit in your house, when you walk by the way, when you lie down, and when you rise up. (NKJV)

Yeshua rebuked the Pharisees for misusing or misinterpreting the Torah.

Joh 5:39 "You search the Scriptures, for in them you think you have eternal life; and these are they which testify of Me. (NKJV)

Luk 11:39 Then the Lord said to him, "Now you Pharisees make the outside of the cup and dish clean, but your inward part is full of greed and wickedness. 40 "Foolish ones! Did not He who made the outside make the inside also? 41 "But rather give alms of such things as you have; then indeed all things are clean to you. 42 "But woe to you Pharisees! For you tithe mint and rue and all manner of herbs, and pass by justice and the love of God. These you ought to have done, without leaving the others undone. 43 "Woe to you Pharisees! For you love the best seats in the synagogues and greetings in the marketplaces. 44 "Woe to you, scribes and Pharisees, hypocrites! For you are like graves which are not seen, and the men who walk over them are not aware of them." (NKJV)

Mar 7:8 "For laying aside the commandment of God, you hold the tradition of men--the washing of pitchers and cups, and many other such things you do." 9 He said to them, "All too well you reject the commandment of God, that you may keep your tradition. (NKJV)

The Pharisees thought that eternal life was to be found by the act of searching the scriptures. While it is true that all the scriptures testify to Christ, it is not the scriptures but belief in Christ that leads to eternal life. Similarly, following the letter of the law with wrong motives does not lead to righteousness before God. But He doesn't tell them to stop observing Torah. They are to act justly, love God and follow Torah.

C. (*This section refers to the handouts of the first parts of Genesis, Exodus, Numbers and Deuteronomy. The arrows point to the relevant parts of the text.*) Both the Torah and Yeshua command believers to diligently search and study the scripture because it speaks of the Messiah. Not only do the words speak of Messiah, but the very structure of the Torah also points to Messiah. One of the ways that the structure is examined is in looking for first appearances of various elements. In the handout of the first verses of Genesis, locate the first Tav, ת. From there we start counting. Count to the 50th letter after the tav and you arrive at a vav, ו. Another 50 letters after the vav, is a resh, ר, and another 50 to a hey, ה, spelling out Torah. This same pattern is seen in Exodus starting from the first tav, ת in the book of Exodus. In Numbers the pattern is reversed starting with the first hey, ה and going every 50th letter ending with the tav, ת spelling Torah in reverse. In Deuteronomy the pattern is slightly different. It is reversed like that in Numbers but it starts in verse five of chapter 1 with the first hey, ה. It then proceeds with every 49th letter ending at the tav, ת. We don't know exactly why the pattern changes to 49 letters in Deuteronomy. There is an avenue of deeper meaning of scripture when studying the use of numbers and the repeating patterns of numbers in the Torah which we will not explore to any significant depth with this lesson. Perhaps on your own you can look at the patterns of the number 49, which, by the way is seven times seven where seven is the number of spiritual completion.

What is the significance of this pattern? The spacing is important as is the direction the word "Torah" points.

1. Fifty is number of deliverance. The Jubilee Year is every 50th year. The year of Jubilee is the year that all the slaves are freed and debts are canceled. The interval from the Feast of Firstfruits and the Feast of Weeks, also known as Pentecost, is 50 days. (See Leviticus chapter 23 for details.) Yeshua rose from the dead on the Feast of Firstfuits and the Holy Spirit was given on the Feast of Weeks 50 days later. Forty-nine is seven sevens. Seven is the number of completion. God rested on the seventh day and made it holy. Deuteronomy completes the Books of Moses and thus, is a type of completion. It also marks the completion of the wandering in the wilderness.

2. We can look at the word Torah as pointing forward in Genesis and Exodus and pointing backwards in Numbers and Deuteronomy. In a sense the word Torah is an arrow pointing both forward and backward. To what is Torah pointing? It points to the center book of Leviticus. There are two patterns that we see the words Torah pointing to in Leviticus. For the first pattern, look at the handout showing Lev 1:1. Starting with the 2nd letter and counting every eighth letter you get the name of God or Yahovah (YHVH), יהוה (Right to left!)

Hebrew word picture
Jehovah: יהוה
Yood: י Hand
Hey: ה Revealed
Vav: ו Nail
Hey: ה Revealed

Jehovah: The hand revealed the nail revealed.

The number eight is associated with God. You see it repeated many times and places in the scriptures. The number eight is the beginning of a new cycle. For example, there are seven days in a week, and the eighth day is the beginning of a new week, a new cycle. It is the day newborn males are to be circumcised. Another example of eight as a new beginning is in Lev 9:1. It refers to eighth day of the process of setting up the temple sacrifices.

> Le 9:1 It came to pass on the eighth day that Moses called Aaron and his sons and the elders of Israel. (NKJV)

3. For the second pattern, we look at the exact center words of the five books of Moses, the Torah proper. There are 79,848 Hebrew words in the books of Moses, an even number. The following verse in Leviticus contains the center two words. Specifically the center falls between the words translated as "searched" and "carefully."

> Le 10:16a But Moses **searched carefully** for the goat of the sin offering, and behold, it had been burned up!... (NASB)

In the original Hebrew text the words translated to "searched carefully" are a double verb. That is, the same word repeats but in a different tense. In the ancient and biblical Hebrew, there are no vowels, only consonants and thus, the two words look and are spelled the same but are pronounced differently with the vowel sounds implied by context. The pronunciation is "darosh, darash." If translated literally it would be "searching, he searched." Thus, both sides of the center of the Torah have the same word instructing us to search.

Search: #1875. דרש darash, daw-rash' a primitive root; properly, to tread or frequent; usually to follow (for pursuit or search); by implication, to seek or ask; specifically to worship:-- X diligently, inquire, make inquisition, question, require, search, seek (for, out).

The use of a double verb is a Hebrew linguistic idiom that adds extra importance and/or a deeper meaning to the word or phrase. It is sometime used in English as well to give extra importance or emphasis, such as "Run, run!" Its use gives an added intensity to the phrase where it is used. The repeated use of the word search in the exact center of the Torah teaches us that the entire Torah revolves around constant studying and searching. We should never stop studying and seeking an ever deeper and broader understanding of the Word of God.

D. As we look at the broader context of the scripture in Leviticus 10:16, we see that Moses was searching diligently for something. What was Moses searching for? He was searching for the goat of the sin offering for the people of Israel! We find that the very center of the Torah is about searching for the sin offering.

> Joh 5:39 "You search the Scriptures, for in them you think you have eternal life; and these are they which testify of Me. (NKJV)

> 2 Co 5:21 For He made Him who knew no sin to be sin for us, that we might become the righteousness of God in Him. (NKJV)

Yeshua says the scriptures testify of Him. So, like Moses, we search the Torah diligently, seeking the sin offering, which is Yeshua. We search the beautifully crafted scroll, the Torah, for the shadows of the Messiah.

E. One of the ways we can search the Torah besides the significance and patterns of numbers, is through the names. Names in the Bible have meaning beyond being simply a name. As an example, when we look at the meaning of the names of the ten generations from Adam to Noah found in Genesis chapter 5, we find an interesting message hidden in the meaning of these names spanning a thousand years of history. This also illustrates the importance of at least some understanding of the original Hebrew language.

Adam: Mankind
> #120: 'adam (aw-dawm') from 119; ruddy i.e. a human being (an individual or the species, mankind, etc.

Seth: Is appointed to
> #8352. Sheth, (shayth) from 7896; put, i.e. substituted;
> #7896. shiyth, (sheeth) a primitive root; to place (in a very wide application):-- apply, appoint, array, bring, consider, lay (up), let alone

Enos: Feeble, frail, mortality
> #582. 'enowsh, en-oshe' a mortal (and thus differing from the more dignified 120); hence, a man in general (singly or collectively):
> #605. 'anash, aw-nash' a primitive root; to be frail, feeble

Cainan: A fixed Dwelling place
> #7018. Qeynan, kay-nawn' from the same as 7064; fixed
> #7064. qen, kane contracted from #7077; a nest (as fixed), sometimes including the nestlings; figuratively, a chamber or dwelling:--nest, room.

Mahalaleel: God who is praised
> #4111. Mahalal'el, mah-hal-al-ale' from 4110 and 410; praise of God

Jared: Comes down, descends
> #3382. Yered, yeh'-red from 3381; a descent
> #3381. dry yarad, yaw-rad' a primitive root; to descend

Enoch: To instruct, train up
> #2585. Chanowk, khan-oke' from 2596; initiated
> #2596. chanak, khaw-nak' a primitive root; properly, to narrow (compare 2614); figuratively, to initiate or discipline:--dedicate, train up.

Methusalah: A man sent forth
> #4968. Methuwshelach, (meth-oo-sheh'-lakh) from 4962 and 7973; man of a dart
> #4962 math, math from the same as 4970; properly, an adult (as of full length); by implication, a man
> #7973. shelach, from 7971; a missile of attack #7971. shalach, (shaw-lakh') a primitive root; to send away, for, or out

Lamech: To be beaten, smitten, and tortured
> #3929 from #4347. makkah, mak-kaw' or (masculine) makkeh {muk-keh'}; (plural only) from 5221; a blow; by implication, a wound; figuratively, carnage, also pestilence:--beaten, blow, plague, slaughter, smote, X sore, stripe, stroke, wound((-ed))

Noah: Bringing rest, a quiet peace
> #5146 Noach, (no'-akh) the same as 5118; rest
> #5118 nuwach, (noo'-akh) or nowach {no'-akh}; from 5117; quiet

When the meanings of these names are placed in a sentence in their original order, it reads:
Mankind/ is appointed to/ feeble, frail, morality/ a fixed dwelling place/ God who is praised/ comes down/ to instruct/ as a man sent forth/ to be beaten smitten and tortured/ bringing rest, a quiet peace.

Here we have the gospel message of Yeshua presented in the names of the 10 generations from the creation of the world! Four thousand years before Yeshua came to secure our redemption, the prophecy was given! The Messiah is hidden throughout the Torah; it is our duty to seek Him.

> Pr 25:2 It is the glory of God to conceal a matter, But the glory of kings is to search out a matter. (NKJV)

Search, search the word of God! Just as Paul admonished Timothy, study to show yourself approved as well. In this day and age of computers and on-line resources, we have at our disposal a vast amount of tools unheard of only a few short years ago. The scriptures are full of richness and depth that we can only imagine the possibilities of what we can find!

16

Student Notes for Searching God's Word

The commandment to study God's word: (2Tim 2:15, 2Tim 3:16-17)

A. What is the Torah? (1Co 14:21)

Torah: #8451. תורה towrah, to-raw' or torah {to-raw'}; from 3384; a precept or statute, especially the Decalogue or Pentateuch:--law.

#3384. ירה yarah, yaw-raw', yara; {yaw-raw'}; a primitive root; properly, to flow as water (i.e. to rain); transitively, to lay or throw (especially an arrow, i.e. to shoot); figuratively, to point out (as if by aiming the finger), to teach:--(+) archer, cast, direct, inform, instruct, lay, shew, shoot, teach(-er,-ing), through.

  1. There is an interesting connection between the words Torah and sin. Sin is the Hebrew word chattah.

  Sin: #2403. חטאה chatta'ah, khat-taw-aw' from 2398; an offence (sometimes habitual sinfulness), and its penalty, occasion, punishment (of sin), purifying(-fication for sin)

  #2398. חטא chata', khaw-taw' a primitive root; properly, **to miss**; hence (figuratively and generally) to sin; by inference, to forfeit, lack, expiate, repent, (causatively) lead astray, condemn:-- loss, miss, (make) offend(-er), offer for sin, purge, purify (self).

  Torah:

  Sin: (1 John 3:4)

Hebrew word picture: Hebrew is read right to left
Torah: תורה
Tav: ת Cross, covenant or sign of the covenant
Vav: ו Nail, tent peg, to secure
Resh: ר Person especially the highest person, head
Hey: ה Reveal. At the end of a word hey can mean what comes from or out of, belonging to

Torah: The covenant secured by the highest person revealed or that which comes from the highest person nailed to the cross.

B. The study of the Torah is one of the commandments of the Torah. (De. 6:7, Joh 5:39, Lu 11:39-44, Mar 7:8)

C. The structure of Torah: (Refer to handouts of Genesis, Exodus, Numbers and Deuteronomy)

    1. Fifty is the number of _____.

     Forty-nine is the number of _____

    2. Pointing forward, pointing backward (Refer to handout for Le 1:1)

Hebrew word picture

Jehovah: יהוה

Yood: י Hand

Hey: ה Revealed

Vav: ו Nail

Hey: ה Revealed

Jehovah: The hand revealed the nail revealed.

3. The center of Torah (Lev. 10:16)

Searching, he searched: darosh, darash.

Search: #1875. דרש darash, daw-rash' a primitive root; properly, to tread or frequent; usually to follow (for pursuit or search); by implication, to seek or ask; specifically to worship:-- X diligently, inquire, make inquisition, question, require, search, seek (for, out).

D. What was Moses searching for? (John 5:39, 2 Cor. 5:21)

E. The message in the 10 generations.

Adam: _____
    #120: 'adam (aw-dawm') from 119; ruddy i.e. a human being (an individual or the species, mankind, etc.

Seth: _____
    #8352. Sheth, (shayth) from 7896; put, i.e. substituted;
      #7896. shiyth, (sheeth) a primitive root; to place (in a very wide application):--apply, appoint, array, bring, consider, lay (up), let alone

Enos: _____
    #582. 'enowsh, en-oshe' a mortal (and thus differing from the more dignified 120); hence, a man in general (singly or collectively):
    #605. 'anash, aw-nash' a primitive root; to be frail, feeble

Cainan: _____
    #7018. Qeynan, kay-nawn' from the same as 7064; fixed
    #7064. qen, kane contracted from #7077; a nest (as fixed), sometimes including the nestlings; figuratively, a chamber or dwelling:--nest, room.

Mahalaleel: _____
    #4111. Mahalal'el, mah-hal-al-ale' from 4110 and 410; praise of God

Jared: _____
    #3382. Yered, yeh'-red from 3381; a descent
    #3381. dry yarad, yaw-rad' a primitive root; to descend

Enoch: _____
    #2585. Chanowk, khan-oke' from 2596; initiated
    #2596. chanak, khaw-nak' a primitive root; properly, to narrow (compare 2614); figuratively, to initiate or discipline:--dedicate, train up.

Methusalah: _____
    #4968. Methuwshelach, (meth-oo-sheh'-lakh) from 4962 and 7973; man of a dart
    #4962 math, math from the same as 4970; properly, an adult (as of full length); by implication, a man
    #7973. shelach, from 7971; a missile of attack #7971. shalach, (shaw-lakh') a primitive root; to send away, for, or out

Lamech: _____
    #3929 from #4347. makkah, mak-kaw' or (masculine) makkeh {muk-keh'}; (plural only) from 5221; a blow; by implication, a wound; figuratively, carnage, also pestilence:--beaten, blow, plague, slaughter, smote, X sore, stripe, stroke, wound((-ed))

Noah: _____
    #5146 Noach, (no'-akh) the same as 5118; rest
    #5118 nuwach, (noo'-akh) or nowach {no'-akh}; from 5117; quiet

Mankind/ is appointed to/ feeble, frail, morality/ a fixed dwelling place/ God who is praised/ comes down/ to instruct/ as a man sent forth/ to be beaten smitten and tortured/ bringing rest, a quiet peace.

The Messiah is hidden throughout scripture; it is our duty to seek Him. (Prov. 25:2)

Genesis 1:1-5

פרשת בראשית

בראשית ברא אלהים את השמים ואת הארץ והארץ
היתה תהו ובהו וחשך על פני תהום ורוח אלהים
מרחפת על פני המים ויאמר אלהים יהי אור ויהי
אור וירא אלהים את־האור כי־טוב ויבדל אלהים בין
האור ובין החשך ויקרא אלהים | לאור יום ולחשך
קרא לילה ויהי ערב ויהי בקר יום אחד

Exodus 1:1-7

פרשת שמות

ואלה שמות בני ישראל הבאים מצרימה את יעקב
איש וביתו באו ראובן שמעון לוי ויהודה יששכר
זבולן ובנימן דן ונפתלי גד ואשר ויהי כל נפש יצאי
ירך יעקב שבעים נפש ויוסף היה במצרים וימת יוסף
וכל אחיו וכל הדור ההוא ובני ישראל פרו וישרצו

Numbers 1:1-4

פרשת במדבר

וידבר יהוה אל משה במדבר סיני באהל מועד באחד
לחדש השני בשנה השנית לצאתם מארץ מצרים
לאמר שאו את ראש כל עדת בני ישראל למשפחתם
לבית אבתם במספר שמות כל זכר לגלגלתם מבן
עשרים שנה ומעלה כל יצא צבא בישראל תפקדו
אתם לצבאתם אתה ואהרן ואתכם יהיו איש איש

Deuteronomy 1:5-8

פרשת דברים

בארץ מואב הואיל משה באר את התורה הזאת
לאמר יהוה אלהינו דבר אלינו בחרב לאמר רב לכם
שבת בהר הזה פנו וסעו לכם ובאו הר האמרי ואל
כל שכניו בערבה בהר ובשפלה ובנגב ובחוף הים
ארץ הכנעני והלבנון עד הנהר הגדל נהר פרת ראה
נתתי לפניכם את הארץ באו ורשו את הארץ אשר

Leviticus 1:1

פרשת ויקרא

ויקרא אל משה וידבר יהוה אליו מאהל מועד לאמר

Leviticus 10:16

וחזה התנופה על אשי החלבים יביאו להניף תנופה
לפני יהוה והיה לך ולבניך אתך לחק-עולם כאשר
צוה יהוה ואת שעיר החטאת דרש דרש משה והנה
שרף ויקצף על אלעזר ועל איתמר בני אהרן
הנותרם לאמר מדוע לא אכלתם את החטאת
במקום הקדש כי קדש קדשים הוא ואתה נתן לכם

Discussion Questions for Searching God's Word

1. How is the Torah much more than just "law?" What are the implications of the word picture of Torah? Discuss the relationship between Torah and sin.

2. Discuss the relationship between faith, knowledge of the scriptures and deeds. Support your position with scripture.

3. The word Torah points to the center of the Torah containing the Hebrew words literally translated as "searching, he searched." What are some of the things we should search for when reading the scriptures?

4. The word Torah pointed to the name of God, יהוה or Yehovah, and to the sin offering. How are these related?

5. What are the advantages of looking at the scriptures in the original Hebrew language?

6. The Bible is the inspired word of God; as such there are no superfluous words. What is the importance of names in the Bible? How do they show a deeper level of meaning in the scriptures?

The Second Adam

How is Adam like Messiah? Adam is like Messiah in his relationship with Eve. He is also like Adam in that both were created without sin. Yeshua, as the child of God and Mary, was not of the seed of Adam and, thus, was born without sin. Unlike Adam, Yeshua chose to be obedient to God. Through His obedience, we have access to eternal life.

In Romans 5, Paul speaks of Messiah as a second Adam explaining that Adam was a type of Messiah.

> Ro 5:14 Nevertheless death reigned from Adam to Moses, even over those who had not sinned according to the likeness of the transgression of Adam, who is a type of Him who was to come. (NKJV)

Hebrew word pictures: Hebrew is read right to left.

Adam: אדם means ruddy, human being, mankind

Aleph: א   first

Mem-dalet: דם   blood

Adam was the first man literally the "First blood."

Earth (a-da-mah): אדמה

Hey: ה Reveal

Adam: אדם

Adam revealed. Adam was taken out of the earth. (Gen. 2:7)

Mem is depicted either ם when at the end of a word or מ elsewhere in a word.

A. Believers in Messiah are described as being Yeshua's Bride. The model of the marriage relationship can be taken from the creation of Eve. Eve was created from Adam for Adam.

> Ge 2:23 And Adam said, This is now bone of my bones, and flesh of my flesh: she shall be called Woman, because she was taken out of Man. (NKJV)

Paul describes the church as being part of Messiah's body.

> Eph 5:29 After all, no one ever hated his own body, but hc feeds and cares for it, just as Christ does the church-- 30 for we are members of his body. (NIV)

Adam was put into a deep sleep to bring forth his bride. Yeshua was put into the sleep of death and brought new life to all those who believe. And those who believe are His bride. The name Eve (Chavah) means "living."

> Ge 2:21 So the LORD God caused the man to fall into a deep sleep; and while he was sleeping, he took one of the man's ribs and closed up the place with flesh. 22 Then the LORD God made a woman from the rib he had taken out of the man, and he brought her to the man. (NIV)

> Ro 6:4 We were therefore buried with him through baptism into death in order that, just as Christ was raised from the dead through the glory of the Father, we too may live a new life. (NIV)

Hebrew word picture:

Eve: Chavva: חוה

Chet: ח 8th letter. It begins a new cycle of 7, and thus stands for new beginnings or new life.

Vav: ו   the nail or peg, secures, connects

Hey: ה   open window, to reveal, behold

Eve is the revelation of new life secured.

Because Eve was part of his flesh, he would cleave to her. Yeshua cleaves to us!

> Ge 2:24 Therefore shall a man leave his father and his mother, and shall cleave unto his wife: and they shall be one flesh. (KJV)

> Ro 8:38 For I am convinced that neither death nor life, neither angels nor demons, neither the present nor the future, nor any powers, 39 neither height nor depth, nor anything else in all creation, will be able to separate us from the love of God that is in Christ Jesus our Lord. (NIV)

The word "cleave" is from the Hebrew word dabaq.

Cleave: #1692 דבק dabaq *daw-bak'* A primitive root; properly to *impinge*, that is, *cling* or *adhere*; figuratively to *catch* by pursuit: - abide, fast, cleave (fast together), follow close (hard, after), be joined (together), keep (fast), overtake, pursue hard, stick, take.

In Hebrew, the word has a primary meaning but the secondary meanings add depth to the passage. If we look at dabaq as to catch by pursuit, we see an additional meaning. The man pursues the woman in a relationship. They seem to be hardwired that way. Yeshua also pursues us. We don't pursue Him.

1Jo 4:9 In this the love of God was manifested toward us, that God has sent His only begotten Son into the world, that we might live through Him. 10 In this is love, not that we loved God, but that He loved us and sent His Son to be the propitiation for our sins. (NKJV)

Ro 3:10 (Quoting Psalm 14:1-3) As it is written: "There is no one righteous, not even one; 11 there is no one who understands, no one who seeks God. 12 All have turned away, they have together become worthless." (NIV)

Dabaq in its primary meaning to join together is echoed in the instructions of Moses to the Israelites.

De 10:20 Thou shalt fear the LORD thy God; him shalt thou serve, and to him shalt thou **cleave**, and swear by his name. (KJV)

How are we to cleave to God? The Jewish sages taught that by "cleaving" to a teacher of Torah, that is becoming his disciple, they could connect with God through that teacher. A disciple of a teacher would literally live with the teacher learning by observing his life as well as by listening to his teaching. In a sense, they were right. If we cleave to the teacher, Yeshua, we will be joined not only to Christ but through Him to God.

Eph 5:31 For this cause shall a man leave his father and mother, and shall be joined unto his wife, and they two shall be one flesh. 32 This is a great mystery: but I speak concerning Christ and the church. (KJV)

Joh 15:5 I am the vine, you are the branches. He who abides (dabaq) in Me and I in Him, bears much fruit; for without Me you can do nothing. (NKJV)

Joh 15:10 If you keep My commandments, you will abide (dabaq) in My love, just as I have kept My Father's commandments and abide (dabaq) in His love. (NKJV)

We are to cleave (dabaq) to our bridegroom Yeshua, our Adam, and through him we can fulfill Moses' instructions to cleave to God.

B. Paul contrasts Adam with Messiah in 1 Corinthians. What Adam was incapable of doing because he was of the dust of the earth, Yeshua is able to accomplish because He is from heaven.

1Co 15:45 So it is written: "The first man Adam became a living being"; the last Adam, a life-giving spirit. The spiritual did not come first, but the natural, and after that the spiritual. The first man was of the dust of the earth, the second man from heaven. As was the earthly man, so are those who are of the earth; and as is the man from heaven, so also are those who are of heaven. And just as we have borne the likeness of the earthly man, so shall we bear the likeness of the man from heaven. (NIV)

The following chart shows the comparison Paul makes between Adam and Messiah.

Adam	Messiah
First living man given a spirit (Gen2:7)	Life giving spirit
Natural	Spirit
From the dust of the earth	From heaven
We have borne his likeness	We will bear His likeness

In Romans 7, Paul describes how sin leads to death. It is almost as if Paul was putting himself in Adam's place.

> Ro 7:9 Once I was alive apart from law; but when the commandment came, sin sprang to life and I died. (NIV)

1. The commandment not to eat of the tree of the knowledge of good and evil is given to Adam. Adam had a choice to obey God or to choose his own path.

> Ro 7:7 What shall we say, then? Is the law sin? Certainly not! Indeed I would not have known what sin was except through the law. For I would not have known what coveting really was if the law had not said, "Do not covet." (NIV)

> Ge 2:16 And the LORD God commanded the man, "You are free to eat from any tree in the garden; 17 but you must not eat from the tree of the knowledge of good and evil, for when you eat of it you will surely die." (NIV)

2. Adam is tempted. Although Genesis says it is the woman who is tempted, Adam was with her and he was the one actually given the commandment.

> Ro 7:8 But sin, seizing the opportunity afforded by the commandment, produced in me every kind of covetous desire. For apart from law, sin is dead (NIV note: not fully perceived).

> Ge 3:6a When the woman saw that the fruit of the tree was good for food and pleasing to the eye, and also desirable for gaining wisdom… (NIV)

3. Adam gave in to temptation. He went along with Eve instead of standing for what he knew was right.

> Ro 7:9b but when the commandment came, sin sprang to life and I died. (NIV)

> Ge 3:6b …she took some and ate it. She also gave some to her husband, who was with her, and he ate it. (NIV)

4. Death came to Adam. If Adam had obeyed the commandment, he would have had continued access to the tree of life.

Ro 7:10 I found that the very commandment that was intended to bring life actually brought death. (NIV)

Ge 3:22 And the LORD God said, "The man has now become like one of us, knowing good and evil. He must not be allowed to reach out his hand and take also from the tree of life and eat, and live forever." (NIV)

5. Adam blamed anyone but himself. He first blames Eve and indirectly blames God Himself for giving Eve to him in the first place. Adam chose to disobey God—he didn't eat by accident. Paul, in his discourse in Romans, says he was tricked! Satan always tries to trick us.

Ro 7:11 For sin, seizing the opportunity afforded by the commandment, deceived me, and through the commandment put me to death. (NIV)

Ge 3:12 And the man said, The woman whom You gave to be with me, she gave me of the tree, and I ate. (MKJV)

Paul says that all men are without excuse for their wicked actions.

Ro 1:18 The wrath of God is being revealed from heaven against all the godlessness and wickedness of men who suppress the truth by their wickedness, 19 since what may be known about God is plain to them, because God has made it plain to them. 20 For since the creation of the world God's invisible qualities-- his eternal power and divine nature-- have been clearly seen, being understood from what has been made, so that men are without excuse. (NIV)

Moses set before the people of Israel two choices—life or death. The same choice is before us. Moses exhorts the people to cling, or cleave to God!

De 30:19 I call Heaven and earth to record today against you. I have set before you life and death, blessing and cursing. Therefore, choose life, so that both you and your seed may live, 20 so that you may love the LORD your God, and that you may obey His voice, and that you may cling (dabaq) to Him. For He is your life and the length of your days, so that you may dwell in the land which the LORD swore to your fathers, to Abraham, to Isaac, and to Jacob, to give them. (MKJV)

6. The commandment is good. It reveals the heart of man. Adam is ashamed.

Ro 7:12 So then, the law is holy, and the commandment is holy, righteous and good. (NIV)

Ge 3:7 Then the eyes of both of them were opened, and they realized they were naked; so they sewed fig leaves together and made coverings for themselves. (NIV)

Adam and Eve recognized the evil they had chosen. Everything changed. They had separated themselves from God and their attitudes about each other changed. They began to hide from each other.

7. Sin's consequence is death. Adam and Eve were removed from the garden of Eden and no longer had access to the tree of life. Cherubim were set to guard the entrance so they could not return.

> Ro 7:13 Did that which is good, then, become death to me? By no means! But in order that sin might be recognized as sin, it produced death in me through what was good, so that through the commandment sin might become utterly sinful. (NIV)

> Ge 3:17 To Adam he said, "Because you listened to your wife and ate from the tree about which I commanded you, 'You must not eat of it,' "Cursed is the ground because of you; through painful toil you will eat of it all the days of your life. 18 It will produce thorns and thistles for you, and you will eat the plants of the field. 19 By the sweat of your brow you will eat your food until you return to the ground, since from it you were taken; for dust you are and to dust you will return." (NIV)

8. Adam could not redeem himself.

> Ro 7:14 We know that the law is spiritual; but I am unspiritual, sold as a slave to sin. (NIV)

> Ge 2:7 the LORD God formed the man from the dust of the ground and breathed into his nostrils the breath of life, and the man became a living being. (NIV)

Adam was formed from the dust. He had no substance that was not God given and God breathed. It was God Himself who gave him the breath of life. It is only God who can redeem him.

9. God promises a redeemer.

> Ro 7:24 What a wretched man I am! Who will rescue me from this body of death? 25a Thanks be to God-- through Jesus Christ our Lord! (NIV)

God told the serpent that one would come who would be of the seed of woman and thus, fully human, but not of the seed of man, who would crush him—A new Adam.

> Ge 3:15 And I will put enmity between you and the woman, and between your offspring (seed) and hers; he will crush (strike) your head, and you will strike his heel." (NIV)

C. Yeshua is a second Adam.
1. He became flesh for us.

Joh 1:14 The Word became flesh and made his dwelling among us. We have seen his glory, the glory of the One and Only, who came from the Father, full of grace and truth. (NIV)

2. He was tempted in every manner like Adam.

Heb 4:15 For we do not have a high priest who is unable to sympathize with our weaknesses, but we have one who has been tempted in every way, just as we are-- yet was without sin.(NIV)

As we look at the temptations Yeshua faced we see that they are just like the temptations Adam faced. Yeshua was taken into the wilderness and faced three tests. In each case, He uses scripture to answer the temptation.

- Lust of the flesh

    Lu 4:3 The devil said to him, "If you are the Son of God, tell this stone to become bread." 4 Jesus answered, "It is written: 'Man does not live on bread alone.'" (NIV)

    Ge 3:6 ...the fruit of the tree was good for food.... (NIV)

- Lust of the eyes

    Lu 4:5 The devil led him up to a high place and showed him in an instant all the kingdoms of the world. 6 And he said to him, "I will give you all their authority and splendor, for it has been given to me, and I can give it to anyone I want to. 7 So if you worship me, it will all be yours." 8 Jesus answered, "It is written: 'Worship the Lord your God and serve him only.'" (NIV)

    Ge 3:6 ...pleasing to the eye... (NIV)

- Pride of life

    Lu 4:9 The devil led him to Jerusalem and had him stand on the highest point of the temple. "If you are the Son of God," he said, "throw yourself down from here. 10 For it is written: "'He will command his angels concerning you to guard you carefully; 11 they will lift you up in their hands, so that you will not strike your foot against a stone.'" 12 Jesus answered, "It says: 'Do not put the Lord your God to the test.'" (NIV)

    Ge 3:6 ...desirable for gaining wisdom... (NIV)

3. Yeshua was obedient to the Father in all His actions. He came to do the Father's will and was obedient even unto death. Here are a few of the many scriptures that testify to Yeshua's motivation and actions.

Joh 5:30 By myself I can do nothing; I judge only as I hear, and my judgment is just, for I seek not to please myself but him who sent me. (NIV)

Mt 26:39 Going a little farther, he fell with his face to the ground and prayed, "My Father, if it is possible, may this cup be taken from me. Yet not as I will, but as you will." (NIV)

Joh 6:38 For I have come down from heaven not to do my will but to do the will of him who sent me. (NIV)

Php 2:8 And being found in appearance as a man, he humbled himself and became obedient to death-- even death on a cross! (NIV)

4. Adam, by his disobedience brought death to all his descendants. But through the obedience and grace of Yeshua, the second Adam, the gift of life was extended to many people ending death's reign over those who believe.

Ro 5:15 But the gift is not like the trespass. For if the many died by the trespass of the one man, how much more did God's grace and the gift that came by the grace of the one man, Jesus Christ, overflow to the many! (NIV)

Student Notes for the Second Adam

In Romans 5, Paul speaks of Messiah as a second Adam explaining that Adam was a type of Messiah.

> Ro 5:14 Nevertheless death reigned from Adam to Moses, even over those who had not sinned according to the likeness of the transgression of Adam, who is a type of Him who was to come. (NKJV)

Hebrew word pictures: Hebrew is read right to left.

Adam: אדם means ruddy, human being, mankind

Aleph: א   first

Mem-dalet: דם   blood

Adam was the first man literally the "First blood."

Earth (a-da-mah): אדמה

Hey: ה Reveal

Adam: אדם

Adam revealed. Adam was taken out of the earth. (Gen. 2:7)

Mem is depicted either ם when at the end of a word or מ elsewhere in a word.

A. Adam's relationship to Eve is like our relationship to Yeshua our Messiah.
1. Eve was created from Adam for Adam. (Ge 2:23, Eph 5:29)

2. Adam was put into a deep sleep to bring forth his bride. (Ge 2:21-22, Ro 6:4) The name Eve (Chavah) means "living."

Hebrew word picture:

Eve: Chavva: חוה

Chet: ח 8th letter. It begins a new cycle of 7, and thus stands for new beginnings or new life.

Vav: ו the nail or peg, secures, connects

Hey: ה open window, to reveal, behold

Eve is the revelation of new life secured.

3. Adam was to cleave to Eve. (Ge 2:24, Ro 8:38-39)

The word "cleave" is from the Hebrew

Cleave: #1692: דבק dabaq: daw-bak' a primitive root; properly, to impinge, i.e. cling or adhere; figuratively, to catch by pursuit:--abide fast, cleave (fast together), follow close (hard after), be joined (together), keep (fast), overtake, pursue hard, stick, take.

   a. Dabaq: to catch by pursuit (1 Joh 4:9-10, Ro 3:10-12)

   b. Dabaq: in its primary meaning to join together is echoed in the instructions of Moses to the Israelites (De 10:20)

How are we to cleave to God? (Ep 5:31-32, Joh 15:5, Joh 15:10)

We are to cleave (dabaq) to our bridegroom Yeshua, our Adam, and through Him we can fulfill Moses' instructions to cleave to God.

B. Paul contrasts Adam with Messiah (1Co 15:45-49)

Adam	Messiah

In Romans 7, Paul describes how sin leads to death. It is almost as if Paul was putting himself in Adam's place. (Ro 7:9)

1. Adam's choice (Ro 7:7, Ge 2:16-17)

2. Adam's temptation (Ro 7:8, Ge 3:6a)

3. Adam's fall (Ro 7:9b, Ge 3:6b)

4. Death came to Adam. (Ro 7:10, Ge 3:22)

5. Adam blamed anyone but himself. (Ro 7:11, Ge 3:12, Ro 1:18-20, De 30:19-20)

6. The commandment is good. (Ro 7:12, Ge 3:7)

7. Sin's consequence is death. (Ro 7:13, Ge 3:17-19)

8. Adam could not redeem himself. (Ro 7:14, Ge 2:7)

9. God promises a redeemer. (Ro 7:24-25a, Ge 3:15)

.

C.) Yeshua is a second Adam.

1. He became flesh for us. (Joh 1:14)

2. He was tempted in every manner like Adam. (Heb 4:15)

The temptations of Yeshua:

- Lust of the flesh (Lu 4:3-4, Ge 3:6)

- Lust of the eyes (Lu 4:5-8, Ge 3:6)

- Pride of life (Lu 4:9-12, Ge 3:6)

3. The obedience of Yeshua… (Joh 5:30, Mat 26:39, Joh 6:38, Php 2:8)

4. …. Leads to life for those who believe

Ro 5:15 But the gift is not like the trespass. For if the many died by the trespass of the one man, how much more did God's grace and the gift that came by the grace of the one man, Jesus Christ, overflow to the many! (NIV)

Discussion Questions for the Second Adam

1. How is the creation of Eve a picture of Yeshua's death and resurrection?

2. Discuss the comparison of Adam clinging to Eve with Yeshua clinging to the congregation of believers.

3. What was the result of Adam's disobedience? What does Yeshua say about obedience and disobedience? (John 14:22-24)

4. Why couldn't Adam redeem himself and, thus, redeem all of mankind?

5. Yeshua's temptations in the wilderness are like the temptations Adam faced. How do we face these same temptations?

6. What is the result of Yeshua's obedience to the Father? Read 1 John. What does John say about our obedience or disobedience?

Cain and Abel

In the story of Cain and Abel, we will look briefly at the sacrifice system and why Cain's sacrifice wasn't accepted. We will then look at how the relationship between Cain and Abel foreshadows Yeshua's crucifixion and the atoning work of His blood.

First, we need to look at the different types of sacrifices and the requirements for the sacrifices. Sacrifices must be brought in a specific order. The order the sacrifices are offered is found in Leviticus.

> Le 9:15 Then he brought the people's offering, and took the goat, which was the sin offering for the people, and killed it and offered it for sin, like the first one. 16 And he brought the burnt offering and offered it according to the prescribed manner. 17 Then he brought the grain offering, took a handful of it, and burned it on the altar, besides the burnt sacrifice of the morning. 18 He also killed the bull and the ram as sacrifices of peace offerings, which were for the people. And Aaron's sons presented to him the blood, which he sprinkled all around on the altar, (NKJV)

The order is:

1. Sin/guilt offering—makes right before God—expiation.
2. Burnt offering/grain offering (freewill offering)—Draw near to God—sanctification.
3. Peace or fellowship offering—Fellowship with God—communion.

A sin offering must come first. A person first has to be right with God and his fellow man before he can draw near to God in a freewill sacrifice.

> Le 4:13 'Now if the whole congregation of Israel sins unintentionally, and the thing is hidden from the eyes of the assembly, and they have done something against any of the commandments of the LORD in anything which should not be done, and are guilty; 14 'when the sin which they have committed becomes known, then the assembly shall offer a young bull for the sin, and bring it before the tabernacle of meeting. 15 'And the elders of the congregation shall lay their hands on the head of the bull before the LORD. Then the bull shall be killed before the LORD. 16 'The anointed priest shall bring some of the bull's blood to the tabernacle of meeting. 17 'Then the priest shall dip his finger in the blood and sprinkle it seven times before the LORD, in front of the veil. (NKJV)

The bull is the sin offering for the entire congregation of Israel as well as for the priests. The king is to bring a male kid of the goat and the common people are to bring a female kid of the goat (Leviticus 4-7).

After the sin offering comes either the burnt offering or grain offering (Leviticus chapters 1, 2, and 6). The Hebrew word is olah from Strong's #5930 meaning to ascend or go up.

The olah offering is from the herd or flock or fowl. It is totally consumed on the altar—all of it goes up to God. It is a voluntary offering.

> Le 1:1 Now the LORD called to Moses, and spoke to him from the tabernacle of meeting, saying, 2 "Speak to the children of Israel, and say to them: 'When any one of you brings an offering (qorban) to the LORD, you shall bring your offering of the livestock-of the herd and of the flock. 3 'If his offering is a burnt sacrifice (olah) of the herd, let him offer a male without blemish; he shall offer it of his own free will at the door of the tabernacle of meeting before the LORD. (NKJV)

The offering written about in Psalm 51 is the olah, the offering totally consumed by God. It is only acceptable when offered by a repentant heart.

> Ps 51:16 For You do not desire sacrifice, or else I would give it; You do not delight in burnt offering.17 The sacrifices of God are a broken spirit, A broken and a contrite heart-These, O God, You will not despise. 18 Do good in Your good pleasure to Zion; Build the walls of Jerusalem. 19 Then You shall be pleased with the sacrifices of righteousness, With burnt offering and whole burnt offering; Then they shall offer bulls on Your altar. (NKJV)

Abraham's offering of Isaac was to be an olah offering. Isaac was given completely to God.

> Ge 22:2 Then He said, "Take now your son, your only son Isaac, whom you love, and go to the land of Moriah, and offer him there as a burnt offering (olah) on one of the mountains of which I shall tell you." (NKJV)

The next offering is a grain offering (Leviticus chapters 2 and 6). The King James Version calls it a meat offering. The Hebrew word is actually mincha from Strong's #4503 meaning gift, offering, present. It is also a voluntary offering.

> Le 2:1 'When anyone offers a grain offering (mincha) to the LORD, his offering shall be of fine flour. And he shall pour oil on it, and put frankincense on it. 2 'He shall bring it to Aaron's sons, the priests, one of whom shall take from it his handful of fine flour and oil with all the frankincense. And the priest shall burn it as a memorial on the altar, an offering made by fire, a sweet aroma to the LORD. (NKJV)

> Le 2:13 'And every offering of your grain offering you shall season with salt; you shall not allow the salt of the covenant of your God to be lacking from your grain offering (mincha). With all your offerings you shall offer salt. 14 'If you offer a grain offering (mincha) of your firstfruits to the LORD, you shall offer for the grain offering of your firstfruits green heads of grain roasted on the fire, grain beaten from full heads. 15 'And you shall put oil on it, and lay frankincense on it. It is a grain offering. 16 'Then the priest shall burn the memorial portion: part of its beaten

grain and part of its oil, with all the frankincense, as an offering made by fire to the LORD. (NKJV)

Both the olah and the mincha offering are described as offerings. The word for offering is qorban from Strong's #7133 meaning that which is brought near. Literally, the offering is "brought near" the altar. Symbolically the one who offers is "brought near" to God. We can see why the sin offering must precede both the olah and mincha offering.

The last offering is the peace offering (Leviticus chapters 3 and 7). The Hebrew word is from Strong's:

#8002 שלם shalam, peace offering which in turn is from Strong's #7999 shalam, shaw-lam' a primitive root; to be safe (in mind, body or estate); figuratively, to be (causatively, make) completed; by implication, to be friendly; by extension, to reciprocate (in various applications):--make amends, (make an) end, finish, full, give again, make good, (re-)pay (again), (make) (to) (be at) peace(-able), that is perfect, perform, (make) prosper(-ous), recompense, render, requite, make restitution, restore, reward, X surely.

The peace offering consists of an animal from the herd or the flock as well as an accompanying offering of unleavened bread. Only part of the offering is burnt on the altar; some is to be given to the priests. The rest is to be eaten by the one offering the shalam, or peace offering, the same day it is offered.

A. Why Cain's sacrifice wasn't accepted

Now that we have a basic understanding of the sacrifices, let's take a few minutes to read the account of Cain and Abel. What type of offering did Cain and Abel bring?

> Ge 4:2b Now Abel was a keeper of sheep, but Cain was a tiller of the ground. 3 And in the process of time it came to pass that Cain brought an offering (mincha) of the fruit of the ground to the LORD. 4 Abel also brought of the firstborn of his flock and of their fat. And the LORD respected Abel and his offering (mincha), 5 but He did not respect Cain and his offering (mincha). And Cain was very angry, and his countenance fell. (NKJV)

The problem with Cain's offering was not that it wasn't a blood offering. Only the sin/guilt offering and olah offerings had to be of an animal. Cain and Abel's sacrifices were both described as mincha offerings or freewill offerings. Freewill sacrifices are offered after the sin or guilt sacrifice; after one has already established a right relationship with God.

Abel was righteous, therefore his sacrifice was acceptable. Further, the sacrifice was "of the firstborn of the flock and of the fat" which is the LORD's portion.

> Le 27:26 'But the firstborn of the animals, which should be the LORD'S firstborn, no man shall dedicate; whether it is an ox or sheep, it is the LORD'S.

The write of Hebrews writes that The very fact that the sacrifice was accepted is the witness that he was righteous.

> Heb 11:4a "...by faith Abel offered to God a more excellent sacrifice than Cain, through which **he obtained witness that he was righteous."** (NKJV)

Cain's offering was not acceptable, but not because it was a grain offering. There were two issues with Cain's offering. One is that it wasn't from the firstfruits. Genesis 4 said Cain brought an offering of fruit or reward of the crop. In contrast Abel brought an offering of the firstborn of his flock. Instead of offering what God required, Cain offered what he chose to offer.

> Le 2:14 'If you offer a grain offering of your firstfruits to the LORD, you shall offer for the grain offering of your firstfruits green heads of grain roasted on the fire, grain beaten from full heads. (NKJV)

> Le 23:10 Speak unto the children of Israel, and say unto them, When ye be come into the land which I give unto you, and shall reap the harvest thereof, then ye shall bring a sheaf of the firstfruits of your harvest unto the priest: (KJV)

Yeshua describes such a person who thinks he is doing good works but is really just pleasing themselves.

> Mat 7:22 "Many will say to Me in that day, 'Lord, Lord, have we not prophesied in Your name, cast out demons in Your name, and done many wonders in Your name?' 23 "And then I will declare to them, 'I never knew you; depart from Me, you who practice lawlessness!' (NKJV)

The second problem with Cain's offering is that his heart was not repentant as stated in Psalm 51. God himself tells Cain what is wrong.

> Ge 4:6 So the LORD said to Cain, "Why are you angry? And why has your countenance fallen? 7 "If you do well, will you not be accepted? And if you do not do well, sin lies at the door. And its desire is for you, but you should rule over it." (NKJV)

If Cain was righteous, God would have accepted his sacrifice. Instead, sin is at the door. God was encouraging Cain to repent and offer the firstfruits. God is not willing that any should perish.

> 2Pe 3:9 The Lord is not slack concerning His promise, as some count slackness, but is longsuffering toward us, not willing that any should perish but that all should come to repentance. (NKJV)

John explains the answer in his epistle.

1Jo 3:10 In this the children of God and the children of the devil are manifest: Whoever does not practice righteousness is not of God, nor is he who does not love his brother. 11 For this is the message that you heard from the beginning, that we should love one another, 12 not as Cain who was of the wicked one and murdered his brother. And why did he murder him? Because his works were evil and his brother's righteous. (NKJV)

Cain already harbors hatred for his brother and it didn't take much for the hatred to erupt into murder as we can see in verse 8.

Ge 4:8 Now Cain talked with Abel his brother; and it came to pass, when they were in the field, that Cain rose up against Abel his brother and killed him. (NKJV)

The word for "talked" is the Hebrew word **amar** from Strong's #559.

Talked: #559. 'amar, aw-mar' a primitive root; to say (used with great latitude):--answer, appoint, avouch, bid, **boast** self, call, certify, **challenge**, **charge**, + (at the, give) **command**(-ment), commune, consider, declare, **demand**,

Cain is not very pleased with his brother. Yeshua speaks about anger between brothers.

Mat 5:22 "But I say to you that **whoever is angry with his brother without a cause** shall be in danger of the judgment. And whoever says to his brother, 'Raca!' shall be in danger of the council. But whoever says, 'You fool!' shall be in danger of hell fire. (NKJV)

Murder begins in the heart. Before the act is committed anger and resentment build up. The sin starts with the thoughts. In Matthew 5:22, Yeshua was paraphrasing the Torah.

Le 19:17 **'You shall not hate your brother in your heart.** You shall surely rebuke your neighbor, and not bear sin because of him. 18 'You shall not take vengeance, nor bear any grudge against the children of your people, but you shall love your neighbor as yourself: I am the LORD. (NKJV)

What did it mean when God told Cain "he should do well" in Genesis 4:6? Yeshua answers that as well.

Mat 5:23 "Therefore if you bring your gift to the altar, and there remember that your brother has something against you, 24 "leave your gift there before the altar, and go your way. First **be reconciled to your brother**, and then come and offer your gift. (NKJV)

Again, this is also addressed in the Torah. Leviticus gives instructions for the guilt offering. This offering is given after an unintentional sin is committed against another person. Restitution must be made before offering the sacrifice for sin. Only then, will the freewill offering be accepted. Cain should have gone to his brother Abel and been reconciled to his brother. Only then would his sacrifice be accepted.

> Le 6:1 And the LORD spoke to Moses, saying: 2 "If a person sins and commits a trespass against the LORD by lying to his neighbor about what was delivered to him for safekeeping, or about a pledge, or about a robbery, or if he has extorted from his neighbor, 3 or if he has found what was lost and lies concerning it, and swears falsely-in any one of these things that a man may do in which he sins: 4 then it shall be, because he has sinned and is guilty, **that he shall restore what he has stolen, or the thing which he has extorted, or what was delivered to him for safekeeping, or the lost thing which he found, 5 or all that about which he has sworn falsely. He shall restore its full value, add one-fifth more to it, and give it to whomever it belongs, on the day of his trespass offering.** 6 And he shall bring his trespass offering to the LORD, a ram without blemish from the flock, with your valuation, as a trespass offering, to the priest. 7 So the priest shall make atonement for him before the LORD, and he shall be forgiven for any one of these things that he may have done in which he trespasses."(NKJV)

The Hebrew word picture for brother shows us what brothers should be to each other.

Hebrew word picture: Hebrew is read right to left.

Brother: ach: אח

Aleph: א Strong

Chet: ח Fence

A brother is a strong fence. They are fences of protection for one another.

Unite: echad: אחד

Chet-Aleph: אח Brother

Dalet: ד Door

Unite is the brother's door, a door that can only be entered by brothers.

B. Abel as a type of Messiah

1. We saw that Hebrews 11:4 described Abel as righteous and, as such, he is a type of Messiah. Yeshua was also righteous as no one else before or since has been. His free will offering was and is acceptable. He is the firstborn Son of God, was without spot or blemish and offered himself freely.

Joh 10:15 Even as the Father knows Me, I also know the Father. And I lay down My life for the sheep. (MKJV)

Heb 4:15 For we do not have a High Priest who cannot sympathize with our weaknesses, but was in all points tempted as we are, **yet without sin**.(NKJV)

2. Abel was killed by sinful man, his brother Cain, who harbored hatred in his heart. The event that precipitated Abel's murder appears to be that Abel's sacrifice was accepted and thus had favor with God. Yeshua, our Righteous One, was killed by sinful men, literally by His brothers, the Pharisees and Sadducees, because Yeshua rebuked them and claimed an intimate relationship with God. The words of Yeshua speaking to the Jewish leaders are reminiscent of God's words to Cain.

Ge 4:7 "If you do well, will you not be accepted? And if you do not do well, sin lies at the door. And its desire is for you, but you should rule over it."

Joh 7:19 "Has not Moses given you the law? Not one of you keeps the law. Why are you trying to kill me?

This is not to be taken as condemnation against all Jews. These are those who were in authority, the chief priests and the Sanhedrin. At this time **all** the believers were Jews many of whom were priests! (Acts 6:7)

3. A Targum is an Aramaic translation of the Tanakh with elaboration and commentary. The word "targum" means translation or interpretation. They were written after the Babylonian Exile because many of the Jews didn't speak Hebrew anymore. There was a partial Targum of the book of Job found at Qumram among the Dead Sea Scrolls. They were not quite regarded as scripture. Scripture was meticulously copied without making any changes. The Targums contained much of the oral tradition interwoven with scripture. The Targum on Genesis chapter 4 elaborates on the story of Cain and Abel saying that the day that Cain murdered Abel was Nisan 14. This day would become Passover, the day that the Passover lamb is slain to prevent the deaths of the firstborn of Israel. Yeshua was crucified on Passover as much as 400 years after this Targum was written.

4. After Abel is murdered, his blood cries out to God.

Ge 4:10 And He said, "What have you done? The voice of your brother's blood cries out to Me from the ground. (NKJV)

Abel's blood cries out for justice. The word for blood here is in the plural. Abel's bloods cry out for justice; not just Abel, but all the generations that would have been born from Abel. Hebrews says that Abel still speaks. Once again, we look at Hebrews 11:4.

Heb 11:4 By faith Abel offered to God a more excellent sacrifice than Cain, through which he obtained witness that he was righteous, God testifying of his gifts; and **through it he being dead still speak.** (NKJV)

Abel's murder brought judgment to Cain.

Ge 4:11So now you are cursed from the earth, which has opened its mouth to receive your brother's blood from your hand."12 "When you till the ground, it shall no longer yield its strength to you. A fugitive and a vagabond you shall be on the earth." (NKJV)

The generation that was alive at the time of Yeshua's crucifixion was to be held accountable. The word generation is from Strongs #1074 meaning age, generation, time or nation.

Lu 11:49 "Therefore the wisdom of God also said, 'I will send them prophets and apostles, and some of them they will kill and persecute,' 50 "that the blood of all the prophets which was shed from the foundation of the world may be required of this generation, 51 "from the blood of Abel to the blood of Zechariah who perished between the altar and the temple. Yes, I say to you, it shall be required of this generation. (NKJV)

5. But this isn't the end of the story. Where Abel's blood was powerless to bring forgiveness, Yeshua's blood "speaks a better word."

Heb 12:23b You have come to God, the judge of all men, to the spirits of righteous men made perfect, 24 to Jesus the mediator of a new covenant, and to the sprinkled blood that speaks a better word than the blood of Abel. (NIV)

What is the better word that Yeshua's blood speaks? Abel cried out for justice but Yeshua spoke forgiveness.

Lu 23:34 Then Jesus said, "Father, forgive them, for they do not know what they do." And they divided His garments and cast lots. (NKJV)

This plea for God to forgive them for killing Him is more than we realize. Yes, Yeshua's death was necessary and ordained from the beginning of the world. Yes, there is forgiveness for all who call on His name including those who consented to His death and us as well. By stating, "they know not what they do," Yeshua was stating that the sin was an unintentional sin! One that for which, when they discover their sin, restitution is to be made and a sin offering presented.

Le 4:27 'If anyone of the common people sins unintentionally by doing something against any of the commandments of the LORD in anything which ought not to be done, and is guilty, 28 'or if his sin which he has committed comes to his knowledge, then he shall bring as his offering a kid of the goats, a female without blemish, for his sin which he has committed. 29 'And he shall lay his hand on the head of the sin offering, and kill the sin offering at the place of the burnt offering. (NKJV)

The Israelites will one day have their eyes opened and be made aware of their collective sin. They will repent and make restitution. Their sin offering, just like ours, has already been accepted. Yeshua's blood brings eternal life and salvation to all who believe.

Zec 12:10 "And I will pour on the house of David and on the inhabitants of Jerusalem the Spirit of grace and supplication; then they will look on Me whom they pierced. Yes, they will mourn for Him as one mourns for his only son, and grieve for Him as one grieves for a firstborn. 11 "In that day there shall be a great mourning in Jerusalem, like the mourning at Hadad Rimmon in the plain of Megiddo. 12 "And the land shall mourn, every family by itself: the family of the house of David by itself, and their wives by themselves; the family of the house of Nathan by itself, and their wives by themselves; 13 "the family of the house of Levi by itself, and their wives by themselves; the family of Shimei by itself, and their wives by themselves; 14 all the families that remain, every family by itself, and their wives by themselves. 13:1 In that day a fountain shall be opened for the house of David and for the inhabitants of Jerusalem, for sin and for uncleanness." (NKJV)

The fountain that shall be opened is the fountain of the living water!

Jer 2:13 "For My people have committed two evils: They have forsaken Me, the fountain of living waters, And hewn themselves cisterns-broken cisterns that can hold no water." (NKJV)

Joh 4:14 "but whoever drinks of the water that I shall give him will never thirst. But the water that I shall give him will become in him a fountain of water springing up into everlasting life." (NKJV)

Summary: Abel was like a messiah in that he was a righteous man who was killed because of his brother's sin. Yeshua, our righteousness, was killed because of His brother's sins, literally Israel, but globally all mankind. Abel's blood though was incapable of forgiving sin and Cain was forever cursed. Although the generation that saw Yeshua's crucifixion was to be held accountable for not only Yeshua's death but the death of all the prophets including Abel, Yeshua's blood offers forgiveness. His forgiveness is to all who believe including Israel specifically and, globally, all of mankind.

Ro 3:22 This righteousness from God comes through faith in Jesus Christ to all who believe. There is no difference, 23 for all have sinned and fall short of the glory of God, 24 and are justified freely by his grace through the redemption that came by Christ Jesus. 25 God presented him as a sacrifice of atonement, through faith in his blood. (NIV)

48

Cain and Abel Student Notes

In the story of Cain and Abel, we will look briefly at the sacrifice system and why Cain's sacrifice wasn't accepted. We will then look at how the relationship between Cain and Abel foreshadows Yeshua's crucifixion and the atoning work of His blood.

The different types of sacrifices and the requirements for the sacrifices: (Le 9:15-18)

The order is:
  1. Sin/guilt offering: (Le 4:13-17)

  2. Burnt offering/grain offering: (Ps 51:16-19, Ge 22:2, Le 2:1, Le 2:13-16)

Burnt offering: #5930 Olah meaning to ascend or go up.

Grain offering: #4503 Mincha meaning gift, offering, present.

Offering: #7133 Qorban meaning that which is brought near.

3. Peace or fellowship offering: (Le Chapters 3 and 7)

Peace offering: Strong's #8002 shalam, peace offering which in turn is from Strong's #7999 shalam, shaw-lam' a primitive root; to be safe (in mind, body or estate); figuratively, to be (causatively, make) completed; by implication, to be friendly; by extension, to reciprocate (in various applications):--make amends, (make an) end, finish, full, give again, make good, (re-)pay (again), (make) (to) (be at) peace(-able), that is perfect, perform, (make) prosper(-ous), recompense, render, requite, make restitution, restore, reward,

A. Why Cain's sacrifice wasn't accepted

1. What type of sacrifice were Cain and Abel's offerings? (Ge 4:2b-5)

2. Why was Abel's sacrifice acceptable? (Le 27:26, Heb 11:4a)

3. Why wasn't Cain's offering acceptable?

    a. It wasn't _____ (Le 2:14, Le 23:10, Mat 7:22-23)

    b. Cain's heart was not repentant (Ge 4:6-7, 2Pe 3:9, 1Joh 3:10-12)

   c. Cain already harbors hatred for his brother (Ge 4:8, Mat 5:22,
       Le 19:17-18, Mat 5:23-24, Le 6:1-5)

What should brothers be to each other?

Hebrew word picture: Hebrew is read right to left.

Brother: ach: אֶח

Aleph: א Strong

Chet: ח Fence

A brother is a strong fence. They are fences of protection for one another.

Unite: echad: אֶחָד

Chet-Aleph: אֶח Brother

Dalet: ד Door

Unite is the brother's door, a door that can only be entered by brothers.

B. Abel as a type of Messiah
   1. Abel and Yeshua were righteous (Joh 10:15, Heb 4:15)

   2. Abel and Yeshua were killed by sinful man (Ge 4:7, Joh 7:19)

3. The day they died.

A Targum is an Aramaic translation of the Tanakh with elaboration and commentary. The word "targum" means translation or interpretation.

The Targum on Genesis chapter 4:

4. The blood of Abel cries out. (Ge 4:10, Heb 11:4, Ge 4:11-12, Lu 11:49-51)
Generation: #1074 (Greek) meaning age, generation, time or nation.

5. The blood of Yeshua cries out. (Heb 12:23b-24, Lu 23:34, Le 4:27-29, Zec 12:10-13:1, Jer 2:13, Joh 4:14)

His forgiveness is to all who believe including Israel specifically and, globally, all of mankind. (Ro 3:22-25)

Discussion Questions for Cain and Abel

1. The first offering is the sin offering. Read 1 John 1:8-2:2. How does this apply to the sin offering?

2. The second offering is the burnt offering or free will offering given entirely to God with the purpose of drawing near to God. Read 1 John 2:3-6. How do we know that we are "in Him," that is, that we have drawn near to Him?

3. The third offering is the peace or fellowship offering which is a gift to God. Read Romans 12:1-2. What is our gift to God?

4. Psalm 51 describes the unacceptable and acceptable sacrifices. Summarize what these are. How does this apply to why Cain's sacrifice was unacceptable?

5. How important are our relationships with each other when we want to draw near to God? (See also 1 John 4:20-21)

6. Compare the blood of Abel to the blood of Yeshua. How are they alike? How are they opposites?

God Dwells with Man

A. According to Jewish tradition, Adam was created on Tishrei 1 which falls in late September or early October. From Adam's creation until his fall, God dwelt with man. He planted a garden and put Adam in the garden to keep and tend it for Him.

> Ge 2:7 And the LORD God formed man of the dust of the ground, and breathed into his nostrils the breath of life; and man became a living soul. 8 And the LORD God planted a garden eastward in Eden; and there he put the man whom he had formed. (KJV)

The word "formed" is the Hebrew word "yatsar." In verse seven, it has an unusual spelling. The word yatsar is usually spelled יצר, but in verse seven it is spelled וייצר, with an extra yood, י. In ancient Hebrew, the yood is the closed hand signifying actions or deeds. This shows that in the forming of man, God didn't speak him into being; He used both hands and got personally involved in forming Adam. God didn't speak the Garden of Eden into being either; He planted it and placed Adam into it to take care of it for Him.

> Ge 2:15 The LORD God took the man and put him in the Garden of Eden to work it and take care of it. (NIV)

God made a habit of walking in the garden in the evening.

> Ge 3:8 Then the man and his wife heard the sound of the LORD God as he was walking in the garden in the cool of the day, and they hid from the LORD God among the trees of the garden. (NIV)

Adam could eat of anything in the garden except from the tree of the knowledge of good and evil. But Adam and Eve ate from the tree that God told them not to eat from and so He exiled them from His garden.

> Ge 3:22 And the LORD God said, "The man has now become like one of us, knowing good and evil. He must not be allowed to reach out his hand and take also from the tree of life and eat, and live forever." 23 So the LORD God banished him from the Garden of Eden to work the ground from which he had been taken. (NIV)

The Garden of Eden is a special place. Adam was formed from the dust of the earth but not from within the Garden of Eden. God planted the Garden with His own Hands after He formed Adam. He then put Adam into the garden. When God banished Adam from the garden, Adam returned to work the ground from which God made him. He was separated from God and God's dwelling place.

B. At the time of Moses, God created a bridge so He could dwell with man, this time with the nation of Israel. For the first time, God chose an entire nation of people for His own. Since this was a type of new creation, God told Moses that Nisan, the month He would bring the children of Israel out of Egypt, would now be the first month. This calendar starting with Nisan is called the religious or redemption calendar.

> Ex 12:1 The LORD said to Moses and Aaron in Egypt, 2 "This month is to be for you the first month, the first month of your year. (NIV)

The civil calendar still begins with the month of Tishrei. The year numbers continue to change according to the civil calendar because they count from the creation of Adam. In the redemption calendar, Tishrei becomes the seventh month. (See Appendix C: the Biblical Calendar.)

In the month of Nisan, God would redeem the offspring of Abraham, Isaac and Jacob from slavery in Egypt and make them into a holy nation. He would dwell with them. God's presence was with them as a cloud by day and a pillar of fire by night right after they were brought out of Egypt.

> Ex 13:21 By day the LORD went ahead of them in a pillar of cloud to guide them on their way and by night in a pillar of fire to give them light, so that they could travel by day or night. 22 Neither the pillar of cloud by day nor the pillar of fire by night left its place in front of the people. (NIV)

God provided protection from the harsh sun by day and provided light and warmth by night. It must have been an incredible sight to see the cloud covering 2.5 million or more people as well as all their livestock.

This was a time of miraculous provision as well. They had manna for food and water from a rock that followed them through the wilderness. Even their clothing did not wear out!

> De 8:4 "Your garments did not wear out on you, nor did your foot swell these forty years. (NKJV)

God promised to dwell with them and gave instructions for the Israelites to build a tabernacle for Him. The building of the tabernacle began at the Feast of Tabernacles which occurs in the seventh month of the religious calendar. The word tabernacle means temporary dwelling.

> Ex 25:8 "Then have them make a sanctuary for me, and I will dwell among them. (NIV)

The word "among" in this verse can also be translated as within.

Among: #8432. תּוֶךְ tavek, taw'-vek from an unused root meaning to sever; a bisection, the centre:--among(-st), midst (among), with(-in)

God would dwell in the tabernacle in the center of the camp, in their midst. The tribes camped around the tabernacle with three tribes on each side. At a deeper level, we can see that He desires to live within each one of His people.

After they built the tabernacle, the glory of God entered it on Nisan 1.

> Ex 40:17 So the tabernacle was set up on the first day of the first month in the second year. (NIV)

> Ex 40:34 Then the cloud covered the Tent of Meeting, and the glory of the LORD filled the tabernacle. 35 Moses could not enter the Tent of Meeting because the cloud had settled upon it, and the glory of the LORD filled the tabernacle. (NIV)

But this was only a temporary dwelling place. The children of Israel disassembled and reassembled the tabernacle every time they moved camp. In the Song of Moses sung in praise of God after the crossing of the Red Sea, Moses prophesies about a permanent dwelling place for God.

> Ex 15:17 You will bring them in and plant them on the mountain of your inheritance-- the place, O LORD, you made for your dwelling, the sanctuary, O Lord, your hands established. 18 The LORD will reign for ever and ever." (NIV)

God put Adam in the Garden of Eden but He will plant the children of Israel on the mountain of His inheritance. They will be rooted or fastened into His land. God would eventually reveal that the mountain of His inheritance is the Temple Mount in Jerusalem. He allowed Solomon to build Him a temple and at the dedication of the temple, the Shekinah glory of God filled the temple just like it filled the tabernacle when Moses dedicated it.

> 1 Ki 8:10 When the priests withdrew from the Holy Place, the cloud filled the temple of the LORD. 11 And the priests could not perform their service because of the cloud, for the glory of the LORD filled his temple. (NIV)

God said that His name, eyes and heart would always be there.

> 2 Chr 7:16 I have chosen and consecrated this temple so that my Name may be there forever. My eyes and my heart will always be there. (NIV)

This dedication of the temple was during the Feast of Tabernacles in the seventh month which is Tishrei. This feast is to remember that God dwelt among them in the very center of their camp in their journeys in the wilderness. And, also, that their dwelling in the wilderness, in spite of all the miraculous provisions, was merely temporary.

> Le 23:42 Live in booths for seven days: All native-born Israelites are to live in booths 43 so your descendants will know that I had the Israelites live in booths when I brought them out of Egypt. I am the LORD your God.'" (NIV)

Their true dwelling place is in the Promised Land. It looked like they were truly taking possession of the Land with the dedication of the temple. Like in the Garden of Eden, they were to tend and keep it. If they did so following all God's commands, the land would produce abundantly. But Israel did not keep God's statutes and commandments and turned to worship other gods. So He scattered Israel among the nations and allowed the temple to be destroyed.

> 2 Chr 7:19 "But if you (plural) turn away and forsake the decrees and commands I have given you (plural) and go off to serve other gods and worship them, 20 then I will uproot Israel from my land, which I have given them, and will reject this temple I have consecrated for my Name. I will make it a byword and an object of ridicule among all peoples. (NIV)

When Judah went into exile, the Glory of God departed from the temple. Ezekiel's vision of this event is recorded in Ezekiel 9 and 10. His vision specifically mentions the departure in chapter 10 verses 18 and 19. His vision was on the fifth of Elul, the sixth month of the religious calendar.

> Eze 8:1 In the sixth year, in the sixth month on the fifth day, while I was sitting in my house and the elders of Judah were sitting before me, the hand of the Sovereign LORD came upon me there. (NIV)

The first of Elul begins a forty-day period of repentance and mourning for one's wrong actions. This forty-day period coincides with Moses' second forty-day sojourn on Mt. Sinai to make atonement for Israel after the sin of the Golden Calf. During these forty days, the children of Israel mourned and repented of their sin.

Ezekiel saw the Shekinah glory leave the temple on the fifth day of the forty-day period.

> Eze 10:18 Then the glory of the LORD departed from over the threshold of the temple and stopped above the cherubim. 19 While I watched, the cherubim spread their wings and rose from the ground, and as they went, the wheels went with them. They stopped at the entrance to the east gate of the LORD's house, and the glory of the God of Israel was above them. (NIV)

At the end of seventy years of exile, Judah returned to the Promised Land and rebuilt the temple, but the scriptures do not record the return of the Shekinah glory to this second temple. Instead God was getting ready to dwell with man in a slightly different way.

C. God again took up temporary dwelling with man when Yeshua took up the temporary tabernacle of human flesh to dwell (tabernacle) with man.

> Joh 1:14 The Word became flesh and made his dwelling among us. We have seen his glory, the glory of the One and Only, who came from the Father, full of grace and truth. (NIV)

Yeshua's specific purpose was to make atonement for man so that man would no longer be separated from God. By the shedding of His blood, we who believe in Him will have eternal life.

> Joh 3:16 "For God so loved the world that he gave his one and only Son, that whoever believes in him shall not perish but have eternal life. 17 For God did not send his Son into the world to condemn the world, but to save the world through him. (NIV)

> 1Jo 4:10 This is love: not that we loved God, but that he loved us and sent his Son as an atoning sacrifice for our sins. (NIV)

> 1Jo 4:14 And we have seen and testify that the Father has sent his Son to be the Savior of the world. (NIV)

We saw in the Song of Moses in Exodus 15, that Jerusalem with the Temple Mount is God's inheritance. How can God who already owns everything inherit anything? Yeshua inherits as the Son of David who sits on David's throne.

> Jer 33:16 In those days Judah will be saved and Jerusalem will live in safety. This is the name by which it will be called: The LORD Our Righteousness.' 17 For this is what the LORD says: 'David will never fail to have a man to sit on the throne of the house of Israel, (NIV)

God's name is still there in Jerusalem. He chose Jerusalem as His inheritance.

> Zec 2:12 The LORD will inherit Judah as his portion in the holy land and will again choose Jerusalem. (NIV)

Now He has provided His Son Yeshua to inherit His portion.

D. Yeshua will return to reign on David's throne. When will this happen? Work on the tabernacle in the wilderness began on the Feast of Tabernacles and the dedication of Solomon's temple was on the Feast of Tabernacles. Yeshua will return again at the Feast of Tabernacles when once again work on the temple will begin!

> Eze 37:24 "'My servant David will be king over them, and they will all have one shepherd. They will follow my laws and be careful to keep my decrees. 25 They will live in the land I gave to my servant Jacob, the land where your fathers lived. They and their children and their children's children will live there forever, and David my servant will be their prince forever. 26 I will make a covenant of peace with them; it will be an everlasting covenant. I will establish them and increase their numbers, and I will put my sanctuary among them forever. 27 My dwelling place will be with them; I will be their God, and they will be my people. 28 Then the nations will know that I the LORD make Israel holy, when my sanctuary is among them forever.'" (NIV)

Yeshua will rebuild the temple. The prophet Zechariah refers to Yeshua as the Branch. Jeremiah refers to him as the Branch of David in chapters 23 and 31.

> Zec 6:12 Tell him this is what the LORD Almighty says: 'Here is the man whose name is the Branch, and he will branch out from his place and build the temple of the LORD. 13 It is he who will build the temple of the LORD, and he will be clothed with majesty and will sit and rule on his throne. And he will be a priest on his throne. And there will be harmony between the two.' (NIV)

Ezekiel records the vision of the Glory of God entering the new temple.

> Eze 40:1 In the twenty-fifth year of our exile, at the beginning of the year, on the tenth of the month, in the fourteenth year after the fall of the city-- on that very day the hand of the LORD was upon me and he took me there. (NIV)

In order to understand when this vision took place, we need to understand what is meant by the phrase "at the beginning of the year."

The phrase "…at the beginning of the year…" in Hebrew reads Rosh Hashanah. This phrase is only used at this one place in the Bible. The usual convention is to state the number of the month. For example in Ezekiel 8:1, we read that Ezekiel's vision of the Shekinah glory departing the temple occurred on the "sixth year, in the sixth month on the fifth day." So, what is the time frame for this vision? We find a phrase similar to "at the beginning of the year" in Exodus 23:16. The phrase is "… at the end of the year..." referring to the Feast of Tabernacles or Ingathering in the month of Tishrei.

> Ex 23:16b "… and the Feast of Ingathering at the end of the year, when you have gathered in the fruit of your labors from the field. (NKJV)

Tishrei is the first month of the civil calendar when the year number changes. Rosh Hashanah is another name for the civil New Year on Tishrei 1. The feasts in the month of Tishrei, the seventh month of the religious calendar, end the feast cycle for the year. The observances of these feasts extend from the 1st to the 22nd of the month. This period of time is regarded as ending one year and beginning the next. It is a sort of twenty-two day New Year's celebration!

So this vision took place on Tishrei 10 on Yom Kippur, the Day of Atonement. The forty days of repentance which began on Elul 1 culminates here on the Day of Atonement. The Shekinah glory of God left the temple on the fifth of Elul some 2500 years ago and will return at the end of this 40-day period of mourning in the year of Yeshua's return.

The Feast of Ingathering or Tabernacles which celebrates God dwelling with the children of Israel in the wilderness begins on Tishrei 15 just 5 days after Yom Kippur and exactly forty days after Elul 5 when the glory left the temple.

Eze 43:1 Then the man brought me to the gate facing east, 2 and I saw the glory of the God of Israel coming from the east. His voice was like the roar of rushing waters, and the land was radiant with his glory. 3 The vision I saw was like the vision I had seen when he came to destroy the city and like the visions I had seen by the Kebar River, and I fell facedown. 4 The glory of the LORD entered the temple through the gate facing east. 5 Then the Spirit lifted me up and brought me into the inner court, and the glory of the LORD filled the temple. 6 While the man was standing beside me, I heard someone speaking to me from inside the temple. 7 He said: "Son of man, this is the place of my throne and the place for the soles of my feet. This is where I will live among the Israelites forever. The house of Israel will never again defile my holy name-- neither they nor their kings-- by their prostitution; and the lifeless idols of their kings at their high places. (NIV)

This time God dwells among them permanently. The cloud of God's Shekinah Glory covers and protects them once again like it did in the wilderness.

Isa 4:5 then the LORD will create above every dwelling place of Mount Zion, and above her assemblies, a cloud and smoke by day and the shining of a flaming fire by night. For over all the glory there will be a covering. 6 And there will be a tabernacle for shade in the daytime from the heat, for a place of refuge, and for a shelter from storm and rain. (NKJV)

At the end of the 1000 year reign of Yeshua, the earth will be made new and God will dwell with man forever on the new earth.

Rev 21:1 Then I saw a new heaven and a new earth, for the first heaven and the first earth had passed away, and there was no longer any sea. 2 I saw the Holy City, the new Jerusalem, coming down out of heaven from God, prepared as a bride beautifully dressed for her husband. 3 And I heard a loud voice from the throne saying, "Now the dwelling of God is with men, and he will live with them. They will be his people, and God himself will be with them and be their God. (NIV)

Student Notes for God dwells with man

A. At creation (Ge 2:7-8, Ge 2:15, Ge 3:8)

Formed: #3335: yatsar: usual spelling: יצר

Spelling in verse seven: וייצר

    a. Sin separated man from God (Ge 3:22-23)

B. At the time of Moses (Ex 12:1-2, Ex 13:21-22, De 8:4, Ex 25:8, Ex 40:17, Ex 40:34-35, Ex 15:17-18))

    a. In the temple in Jerusalem (1Ki 8:10-11, 2Chr 7:16, Le 23:42-43, 2Chr 7:19-20)

    b. The Glory of God departs: (Eze 8:1, Eze 10:18-19)

C. Yeshua comes to dwell with man. (Joh 1:14, Joh 3:16-17, 1Jo 4:10, 14, Jer 33:16-17, Zec 2:12)

D. He is coming again. (Eze 37:24-28, Zec 6:12-13, Eze 40:1, Ex 23:16b, Eze 43:1-7, Isa 4:5-6, Re 21:1-3)

Discussion Questions for God Dwells With Man

1. It has always been God's desire to dwell with man. Discuss how God dwelled or will dwell with man providing for his needs in each of these situations.

    A. In the Garden of Eden

    B. In the Tabernacle in the wilderness

    C. In the temple in Jerusalem

    D. In the body of Yeshua

    E. In our bodies (Joh 15:1-11)

    F. In the millennial reign (Zec 14:8-21)

    G. In the new creation (Isa 65:17-25)

2. What is the result of obedience or disobedience in each situation above?

The Woman Caught in Adultery

John 8:2-11 tells the story of Yeshua being confronted by the Pharisees and teachers of the law with a woman caught in adultery. When questioned about what He would do, Yeshua stooped down and wrote in the earth. When they continued to question him, He stood and replied that the one without sin should throw the first stone. He then bent down and resumed writing in the earth. We can figure out what Yeshua probably wrote by looking at the context of the incident. First, take a few minutes to read John 8:2-11.

This incident occurs as Yeshua is nearing the end of His earthly ministry. Six months from this incident, Judas betrays Him and the High Priest turns Him over to the Romans who crucify Him. At this point in His ministry, masses of people followed Him and believed, at the very least, that He was from God. Many believed that He was the Messiah. But other people including His own brothers did not believe in Him. Those in positions of authority did not believe in Him and feared His influence with the people. They sought for a way to kill him.

> Joh 7:1 After these things Jesus walked in Galilee; for He did not want to walk in Judea, because the Jews sought to kill Him. (NKJV)

This statement reflects the societal and cultural situation of this time. Hersh Goldwurm, In the <u>History of the Jewish People: Second Temple Era,</u> records that civil authority had so far broken down that the Great Sanhedrin, the Jewish "Supreme Court" no longer even held court. Corruption was rampant; mobs ruled the city. Some of the mobs were even in the pay of the priests. The society reflected the worst manifestation of the evils condemned by the prophets. Isaiah writes of God's response to this state of affairs.

> Isa 1:15 When you spread out your hands, I will hide My eyes from you; Even though you make many prayers, I will not hear. Your hands are full of blood. 16 "Wash yourselves, make yourselves clean; Put away the evil of your doings from before My eyes. Cease to do evil, 17 Learn to do good; Seek justice, Rebuke the oppressor; Defend the fatherless, Plead for the widow. (NKJV)

Even though they had a form of godliness going through all the rituals, they were corrupt in all the ways that really mattered. We see that pattern of corruption from the very beginning of Yeshua's ministry when He first goes up to Jerusalem for the Passover and throws out all the moneychangers.

> Joh 2:13 Now the Passover of the Jews was at hand, and Jesus went up to Jerusalem.14 And He found in the temple those who sold oxen and sheep and doves, and the moneychangers doing business. 15 When He had made a whip of cords, He drove them all out of the temple, with the sheep and the oxen, and poured out the changers' money and overturned the tables. 16 And He said to those who sold doves, "Take these things away! Do not make My Father's house a house of merchandise!" (NKJV)

Yeshua didn't object to the Passover and the sacrifices; He objected to the mockery that was made of them.

As we read the events of John chapter 7 leading up to this incident, we see the issue of authority and right judgment coming up again and again. The leaders question where Yeshua got His teaching and His answer questions their own motives, righteousness and judgment.

> Joh 7:16 Jesus answered them and said, "My doctrine is not Mine, but His who sent Me. 17 "If anyone wants to do His will, he shall know concerning the doctrine, whether it is from God or whether I speak on My own authority. 18 "He who speaks from himself seeks his own glory; but He who seeks the glory of the One who sent Him is true, and no unrighteousness is in Him. 19 "Did not Moses give you the law, yet none of you keeps the law? Why do you seek to kill Me?" (NKJV)

Finally, this event occurred at the close of the Feast of Tabernacles on the eighth day which was to be observed as a Sabbath.

> Le 23:36 'For seven days you shall offer an offering made by fire to the LORD. On the eighth day you shall have a holy convocation, and you shall offer an offering made by fire to the LORD. It is a sacred assembly, and you shall do no customary work on it. (NKJV)

John records that this incident occurred after the last day of the feast. The Feast itself is seven days long with the eighth day Sabbath day of rest added on the end.

> Joh 7:37 On the last day, that great day of the feast, Jesus stood and cried out, saying, "If anyone thirsts, let him come to Me and drink. (NKJV)

> Joh 8:2 Now early in the morning He came again into the temple, and all the people came to Him; and He sat down and taught them. (NKJV)

The theme of the Feast of Tabernacles is to rejoice.

> De 16:14 "And you shall rejoice in your feast, you and your son and your daughter, your male servant and your female servant and the Levite, the stranger and the fatherless and the widow, who are within your gates. (NKJV)

A key verse for the Feast was Isaiah 12:3:

> "Therefore with joy you will draw water from the wells of salvation." (NKJV)

The priest conducted an entire ceremony around drawing water out of the wells of salvation during which the priests and the people would circle the altar singing Isaiah 12:3 and Psalms 118 about God's salvation, specifically Psalm 118:25 which says, "Save now, I beseech you, O LORD." On the seventh and last day of the feast, the priests would circle the altar seven times while singing. This last day is referred to by John as the last and greatest day of the feast. It is called Hashana Rabba, literally, the great "save now."

Yeshua's very name is also significant in the context of this ceremony. The English name Jesus is really a transliteration of the Greek Iesous which is a transliteration of the Hebrew Yeshua. Jesus' Hebrew name, the name He was born with is Yeshua. The closest English name to Yeshua is Joshua.

Yeshua: #3442 ישוע yay-shoo'-ah, shortened version of Yehoshua (3091); he will save

Joshua: #3091;יהושע Yehoshua: the LORD saves

Matthew tells us that Yeshua received His name because He would save His people from their sins; He would be their salvation.

> Mat 1:21 NKJV 21 "And she will bring forth a Son, and you shall call His name JESUS, for He will save His people from their sins."

When we look at the word for salvation in Isaiah 12:3, we see that it is the same Hebrew word but in a different tense.

Salvation: #3444. ישועה yesh-oo'-aw something saved, salvation

It was during this ceremony on the seventh day of the feast called Hashana Rabba, when the people are crying out to God for salvation that Yeshua stood up and declared that He was the living water.

> Joh 7:37 On the last day, that great day of the feast, Yeshua stood and cried out, saying, "If anyone thirsts, let him come to Me and drink. 38 He who believes in Me, as the Scripture has said, out of his heart will flow rivers of living water." (NKJV)

Yeshua was declaring that He, whose very name means salvation, was the Messiah! The Psalms and the prophets refer to God's salvation as a fountain of life and a fountain of living waters. In the day that Messiah returns, living waters will flow from Jerusalem.

> Ps 36:7 How precious is Your lovingkindness, O God! Therefore the children of men put their trust under the shadow of Your wings.8 They are abundantly satisfied with the fullness of Your house, And You give them **drink from the river** of Your pleasures. 9 For with You is the **fountain of life**; In Your light we see light. (NKJV)

> Jer 2:13 "For My people have committed two evils: They have forsaken Me, the **fountain of living waters**, And hewn themselves cisterns-broken cisterns that can hold no water. (NKJV)

> Zec 14:8 And in that day it shall be That **living waters** shall flow from Jerusalem, Half of them toward the eastern sea And half of them toward the western sea; In both summer and winter it shall occur. 9 And the LORD shall be King over all the earth. In that day it shall be-"The LORD is one," And His name one. (NKJV)

Zec 13:1 "In that day a **fountain** shall be opened for the house of David and for the inhabitants of Jerusalem, for sin and for uncleanness. (NKJV)

Yeshua's declaration that He was the source of living water was not lost on the teachers of the Law and the Pharisees. They sought to test Him so they could at the very least discredit Him with the people. Hopefully, they could even convict Him in a matter of Law. Jeremiah writes that the Messiah will rule with righteousness and judgment.

Jer 23:5 "Behold, the days are coming," says the LORD, "That I will raise to David a Branch of righteousness; A King shall reign and prosper, And execute judgment and righteousness in the earth. (NKJV)

The incident with the woman caught in adultery occurred the very next day called Shemini Atzerat, the assembly of the eighth day, observed as the Sabbath conclusion to the Feast of Tabernacles. The rejoicing on the eighth day takes the form of the Torah itself rejoicing in God's salvation. It was a day for studying the scriptures, teaching one's disciples, holding discussions among the Rabbis and dancing through the temple with the Torah scroll itself. The Pharisees and teachers of the Law came to Yeshua on this day with the intent to trap him.

Joh 8:6a This they said, testing Him, that they might have something of which to accuse Him. (NKJV)

In doing so, they themselves were violating the Law on at least two points; (1) they only brought the woman for judgment and (2) they didn't bring the witnesses.

Le 20:10 'The man who commits adultery with another man's wife, he who commits adultery with his neighbor's wife, the adulterer and the adulteress, shall surely be put to death. (NKJV)

De 19:15 "One witness shall not rise against a man concerning any iniquity or any sin that he commits; by the mouth of two or three witnesses the matter shall be established. (NKJV)

A third violation is that in Jewish civil law, only the Great Sanhedrin could try a capital case. Since the Sanhedrin was not meeting, no capital cases could be tried. Further, they violated the intent of the rejoicing of the Torah by breaking the Sabbath. On this day on which the Torah itself is said to be rejoicing, they grieved both the written Torah by breaking its commandments and the Living Torah of Yeshua by subverting the Torah to their own ends.

The Pharisees and teachers of the law were at that very moment sinning! When Yeshua says, "He who is without sin among you, let him throw a stone at her first." (John 8:7) and then stooped down and continued to write on the ground (v. 8), what could Yeshua have written in the earth that would cause them to eventually acknowledge that they were sinning?

Jeremiah 17:13 speaks to all of these issues.

> Jer 17:13 O LORD, the hope of Israel, All who forsake You shall be ashamed. "Those who depart from Me Shall be written in the earth, Because they have forsaken the LORD, The fountain of living waters." (NKJV)

First, the hope of Israel is a name for the Messiah.

> Jer 14:8 O the Hope of Israel, his Savior in time of trouble, Why should You be like a stranger in the land, And like a traveler who turns aside to tarry for a night?(NKJV)

> Jer 50:7 All who found them have devoured them; And their adversaries said, 'We have not offended, Because they have sinned against the LORD, the habitation of justice, The LORD, the hope of their fathers.' (NKJV)

> Ac 28:20 "For this reason therefore I have called for you, to see you and speak with you, because for the hope of Israel I am bound with this chain." (NKJV)

> Ps 71:5 For You are my hope, O Lord GOD; You are my trust from my youth. (NKJV)

Yeshua had just the previous day declared that He was the Messiah. Second, they celebrated the ceremony of water pouring rejoicing in the "fountain of living waters" each day during the seven days of the Feast of Tabernacles so Jeremiah 17:13 would be well known to the Pharisees and the teachers of the Law. Perhaps Yeshua was writing this very verse the first time he bent to write in the earth.

Third, the Feast of Tabernacles is actually the third feast celebrated within a three week period. One of the themes for the feasts of Trumpets and Yom Kippur, the two feasts that lead up to the Feast of Tabernacles, was examining one's life to ensure that one's name is written in the Book of Life and not the Book of Death for the coming year. The rejoicing at the Feast of Tabernacles is in God's salvation; that is of being written in the Book of Life. Being written in the earth was the opposite of being written in the Book of Life. When Moses intercedes for Israel after the sin of the golden calf, he pleads that if God cannot forgive His people Israel, that God would blot his name out of God's book.

> Ex 32:32 "Yet now, if You will forgive their sin-but if not, I pray, blot me out of Your book which You have written." (NKJV)

Psalm 69 is accepted as a Psalm about the Messiah. Among its familiar verses are "Zeal for your house consumes me" and "gave me vinegar for my thirst." It also writes about those who are rebellious against God.

> Ps 69:27 Add iniquity to their iniquity, And let them not come into Your righteousness. 28 Let them be blotted out of the book of the living, And not be written with the righteous. (NKJV)

If Yeshua really was the Messiah, by their misuse of Torah they were forsaking God and He had the authority to write their names in the earth blotting their names out of the book of the living. Essentially, they would be cut off from their God and their people a consequence of eternal significance. In seeking to trap Yeshua, they only succeeded in trapping themselves. One by one, the accusers left leaving only Yeshua who is not our accuser but our intercessor.

> Heb 7:25 Therefore He is also able to save to the uttermost those who come to God through Him, since He always lives to make intercession for them. (NKJV)

> Joh 8:11 And Jesus said "Neither do I condemn you. Go and sin no more" (NKJV).

Once again, Yeshua proved Himself as the Messiah executing righteousness and judgment. One aspect of judgment and righteousness is mercy and forgiveness. When God proclaimed His name to Moses after the children of Israel sinned by building and worshipping the golden calf, mercy and forgiveness are the first qualities mentioned.

> Ex 34:6 And the LORD passed before him and proclaimed, "The LORD, the LORD God, merciful and gracious, longsuffering, and abounding in goodness and truth, 7 "keeping mercy for thousands, forgiving iniquity and transgression and sin, by no means clearing the guilty, visiting the iniquity of the fathers upon the children and the children's children to the third and the fourth generation." (NKJV)

It is only after mercy and longsuffering are exhausted that judgment takes place. Peter tells us that God wants everyone to come to repentance.

> 2Pe 3:9 The Lord is not slack concerning His promise, as some count slackness, but is longsuffering toward us, not willing that any should perish but that all should come to repentance. (NKJV)

Yeshua Himself said that He came to call the sinners to repentance but when He comes again, it will be for salvation for those who love Him and judgment for those who don't.

> Joh 3:18 "He who believes in Him is not condemned; but he who does not believe is condemned already, because he has not believed in the name of the only begotten Son of God. (NKJV)

Student Notes for the Woman Caught in Adultery

John 8:2-11 tells the story of Yeshua being confronted by the Pharisees and teachers of the law with a woman caught in adultery. When questioned about what He would do, Yeshua stooped down and wrote in the earth. We can figure out what Yeshua probably wrote by looking at the context of the incident.

A. It occurred near the end of Yeshua's earthly ministry. (Joh 7:1)

The societal and cultural situation was one of broken down civil authority (Isa 1:15-17, Joh 2:13-16, Joh 7:16-19)

B. At the time of the Feast of Tabernacles (Le 23:36, Joh 7:37, Joh 8:2)

The theme of the Feast of Tabernacles is_____ (Deu 16:14)

The ceremony of water pouring (Isa 12:3)

Yeshua #3442: ישוע   shortened version of Yehoshua (#3091); he will save

Joshua #3091: יהושע   Yehoshua: the LORD saves (Mat 1:21)

Salvation: #3444. ישועה   yesh-oo'-aw something saved, salvation

Yeshua declared He was _____ (Joh 7:37-38)

This is a name for the _____ (Ps 36:7-9, Jer 2:13, Zec 14:8-9, Zec 13:1)

C. The eighth day of the Feast of Tabernacles:

The Pharisees and teachers of the Law violated the Torah: (Jer 23:5, Joh 8:6a)

    1. (Le 20:10)

    2. (De 19:15)

They violated the intent of the day!

What could Yeshua have written in the earth to make them acknowledge that they were at that very moment sinning? (Jer 17:13)
1. The Hope of Israel is a name for _____(Jer 14:8, Jer 50:7, Ac 28:20, Ps 71:5)

2. The Ceremony of the water Pouring

3. Written in the Book of Life (Ex 32:32, Ps 69:27-28)

If Yeshua really was the Messiah, _____

He probably wrote their names in the earth!

Yeshua is not our accuser but our intercessor (Heb 7:25, Joh 8:11, Ex 34:6-7, 2Pe 3:9, Joh 3:18)

Discussion Questions for the Woman Caught in Adultery

1. Yeshua's influence among the common people was huge at this time. How does He reveal Himself to them as the Messiah through the rituals of the Feast of Tabernacles?

2. The cry "Hosanna" means save now. How does the meaning of Yeshua's name fit with the rituals of the Feast of Tabernacles?

3. Jeremiah 2:13 contrasts the fountain of living water with broken man-made cisterns. How does this point out the contrast between Yeshua and the Pharisees and Sadducees?

4. In trying to entrap Yeshua into breaking the Torah, the Pharisees and Sadducees themselves broke the Torah. Compare this situation with the good and bad shepherds described in Ezekiel 34.

5. The prophets frequently refer to Israel as an adulterous wife. How does Yeshua's handling of this whole incident illustrate the promise of redemption for Israel?

6. Yeshua's words to the woman to "sin no more" following His statement that He would not accuse her remind us of our own salvation. How should we behave now that we have experienced forgiveness of our sins? (Ro 6:1-2)

7. God says that those who depart from Him will be written in the earth. Compare this with His words to Adam in Genesis 3:19-21 and His actions in regards to Korah in Numbers 16:28-34. Can you find other situations in scripture with this same theme?

In the Time of Noah: Noah as a type of Messiah

A. We have learned that the meaning of names is important in the Bible. The story of Noah begins with his name and its meaning.

Noah's name is also a title for Messiah. Noah's name is from Strong's #5146 which means a quiet peace. It comes from #5118 meaning to give rest or comfort.

> Ge 5:29 And he called his name Noah, saying, "This one will comfort us concerning our work and the toil of our hands, because of the ground which the LORD has cursed." (NKJV)

We see right away that Noah is a type of Messiah. He provides comfort or peace in the midst of a wicked world as well as assurance that a redeemer is coming to redeem man from the curse afflicted on man because of Adam's sin.

Yeshua also promises us rest. We find rest in taking on His yoke.

> Mat 11:29 "Take My yoke upon you and learn from Me, for I am gentle and lowly in heart, and you will find rest for your souls. (NKJV)

He promised us the Holy Spirit as our rest and comforter.

> Joh 14:26 But the Comforter, the Holy Spirit whom the Father will send in My name, He shall teach you all things and bring all things to your remembrance, whatever I have said to you. 27 Peace I leave with you, My peace I give to you. Not as the world gives do I give to you. Let not your heart be troubled, neither let it be afraid. (MKJV)

The word picture of the name Noah emphasizes the promise of a redeemer providing new life as well as comfort in the midst of trouble.

Hebrew word picture: Hebrew is read right to left.

Noah: No-ach': נח

Noon: נ life

Chet: ח the eighth letter. It begins a new cycle of seven, and thus stands for new beginnings.

Noah is the beginning of new life.

> Hebrew word picture: Hebrew is read right to left.
>
> Comforter: me-nach-em: מנחם
>
> Mem: מ Water
>
> No-ach: נח a quiet peace
>
> Mem: ם Water
>
> *The mem is written as ם at the end of a word and מ everywhere else in a word.
>
> The comforter is a quiet peace in the midst of the waters.

B. Right after learning Noah's name, we learn that he was righteous in an evil generation and was the heir of righteousness.

> Ge 6:9 This is the account of Noah. Noah was a righteous man, blameless among the people of his time, and he walked with God. (NIV)

> Heb 11:7 By faith Noah, when warned about things not yet seen, in holy fear built an ark to save his family. By his faith he condemned the world and became heir of the righteousness that comes by faith. (NIV)

Yeshua was righteous and through Him we are the heirs of righteousness.

> Heb 1:8 But about the Son he says, "Your throne, O God, will last for ever and ever, and righteousness will be the scepter of your kingdom. You have loved righteousness and hated wickedness; therefore God, your God, has set you above your companions by anointing you with the oil of joy." {quoting Psalm 45:6,7} (NIV)

> 2Pe 1:1 Simon Peter, a servant and apostle of Jesus Christ, To those who through the **righteousness of our God and Savior Jesus Christ** have received a faith as precious as ours: (NIV)

C. Not only was Noah himself righteous, he preached righteousness to his generation.

> 2Pe 2:5 if he did not spare the ancient world when he brought the flood on its ungodly people, but protected Noah, **a preacher of righteousness**, and seven others; (NIV)

Yeshua's primary message to the people was repentance. He preached righteousness to all generations including the generations leading up to the time of Noah.

> Mat 4:17 From that time on Jesus began to preach, "Repent, for the kingdom of heaven is near." (NIV)

Isa 51:8"For the moth will eat them like a garment, And the grub will eat them like wool. But My righteousness shall be forever, And My salvation to all generations." (NIV)

1Pe 3:18 For Christ died for sins once for all, the righteous for the unrighteous, to bring you to God. He was put to death in the body but made alive by the Spirit, 19 through whom also he went and preached to the spirits in prison 20a who disobeyed long ago when God waited patiently in the days of Noah while the ark was being built. (NIV)

D. The world ignored Noah's preaching about coming judgment. They continued with their every day lives not noticing the evil around them or the sin they themselves were committing. In Noah's time, the people continued to live in their evil ways and brought judgment on themselves.

Ge 6:11 Now the earth was corrupt in God's sight and was full of violence. God saw how corrupt the earth had become, for all the people on earth had corrupted their ways. (NIV)

Mat 24:38 For in the days before the flood, people were eating and drinking, marrying and giving in marriage, up to the day Noah entered the ark; 39 and they knew nothing about what would happen until the flood came and took them all away. That is how it will be at the coming of the Son of Man. (NIV)

Israel, as a nation, rejected Yeshua's message and brought judgment on themselves.

Ac 2:23 This man was handed over to you by God's set purpose and foreknowledge; and you, with the help of wicked men, put him to death by nailing him to the cross.

Isa 53:3 He was despised and rejected by men, a man of sorrows, and familiar with suffering. Like one from whom men hide their faces he was despised, and we esteemed him not. (NIV)

Ps 118:22 The stone the builders rejected has become the capstone; (NIV)

When Yeshua comes again, judgment on the unrighteous will take them by surprise. The world denies that the flood of the Bible ever occurred neither do they acknowledge that God even created the heavens and the earth.

2Pe 3:5 But they deliberately forget that long ago by God's word the heavens existed and the earth was formed out of water and by water. By these waters also the world of that time was deluged and destroyed. (NIV)

Re 3:3 (spoken to the dead church of Sardis) Remember, therefore, what you have received and heard; obey it, and repent. But if you do not wake up, I will come like a thief, and you will not know at what time I will come to you. (NIV)

Some liberal theologies have even rejected the deity of Messiah! Like the church at Sardis, they need to wake up and relearn what the Bible says. Yeshua tells us that the time of His second coming will be like the time of Noah.

Lu 17:26 "Just as it was in the days of Noah, so also will it be in the days of the Son of Man. 27 People were eating, drinking, marrying and being given in marriage up to the day Noah entered the ark. Then the flood came and destroyed them all. 28 It was the same in the days of Lot. People were eating and drinking, buying and selling, planting and building. (NIV)

Lu 17:34 I tell you, on that night two people will be in one bed; one will be taken and the other left. 35 Two women will be grinding grain together; one will be taken and the other left." 36 Two men will be in the field; one will be taken and the other left. 37 "Where, Lord?" they asked. He replied, "Where there is a dead body, there the vultures(eagles) will gather." (NIV)

Although the English indicates one group taken and the other group left, the original Greek words convey a slightly different message. The English word "taken" is translated from the Greek word paralambano, #3880 in Strong's Greek Dictionary, meaning to receive near. The word translated as "left" is from the Greek word aphiemi, #863 in Strong's Dictionary, meaning to send forth. So one person will be received, and the other will not be left but sent away! Neither one stays behind!

Taken: 3880. παραλαμβνω paralambano, par-al-am-ban'-o from 3844 and 2983; to receive near

Left: 863. αφιημι aphiemi, af-ee'-ay-mee to send forth

The apostles asked where, where will they be sent? Yeshua's answer says they will be sent to the place where the eagles are gathered. The eagle is a carrion bird as well as a bird of prey. They will gather together at the site of many dead bodies.

Yeshua uses the phrase "depart from me" in several of His parables when talking about those who are lawless or who work iniquity. In Matthew 7 when He talks about a tree producing good fruit, in Matthew 25 when He talks about separating those who fed, clothed, and visited the brethren in prison from those who did not, and in the parable of the talents, Yeshua sends away those He does not know.

John also writes about this event in Revelation 19:17-21 when God gathers the carrion birds to feast on dead flesh. I don't want to be where the dead bodies are! It sounds like the unrighteous are indeed sent away.

> Re 19:17And I saw an angel standing in the sun, who cried in a loud voice to all the birds flying in midair, "Come, gather together for the great supper of God, 18 so that you may eat the flesh of kings, generals, and mighty men, of horses and their riders, and the flesh of all people, free and slave, small and great." (NIV)

> Rev. 19:21 The rest of them were killed with the sword that came out of the mouth of the rider on the horse, and all the birds gorged themselves on their flesh. (NIV)

Yeshua told a parable about the end of the age in terms of the wheat and the tares. In the parable, the field in which they grow is the world. At the end of the age, Yeshua will reclaim the world as His kingdom which lasts forever.

> Mat 13:30 Let both grow together until the harvest. At that time I will tell the harvesters: First collect the weeds and tie them in bundles to be burned; then gather the wheat and bring it into my barn.'" (NIV)

Again, we read that Yeshua receives near those who belong to Him and sends away those who don't.

In what other way is Yeshua's second coming like the time of the flood? Noah sent out a raven first.

> Ge 8:7 and sent out a raven, and it kept flying back and forth until the water had dried up from the earth. 8 Then he sent out a dove to see if the water had receded from the surface of the ground. 9 But the dove could find no place to set its feet because there was water over all the surface of the earth; so it returned to Noah in the ark. He reached out his hand and took the dove and brought it back to himself in the ark. (NIV)

Unlike the dove, it did not return to the ark but went "to and fro." The raven may have found plenty of dead flesh to feed on. Job speaks about Satan going "to and fro." Peter says he is "seeking whom he may devour."

> Job 1:7 And the LORD said unto Satan, Whence comest thou? Then Satan answered the LORD, and said, From going to and fro in the earth, and from walking up and down in it. (NKJV)

> 1Pe 5:8 Be sober, be vigilant; because your adversary the devil walks about like a roaring lion, seeking whom he may devour. (NKJV)

A raven, like an eagle or a vulture is a carrion bird, eating whatever it can scavenge including the flesh of dead animals. The dove eats primarily fruit, seeds and plants although some species of doves also eat insects and worms. The dove didn't find anything to eat; it continued to return to the ark until it found a green olive branch.

> Ge 8:10 He waited seven more days and again sent out the dove from the ark. 11 When the dove returned to him in the evening, there in its beak was a freshly plucked olive leaf! Then Noah knew that the water had receded from the earth. 12 He **waited** seven more days and sent the dove out again, but this time it did not return to him. (NIV)

Noah stayed in the ark until judgment was complete. Like Noah, we will be hidden in the day of trouble.

> Isa 26:20 Go, my people, enter your rooms and shut the doors behind you; hide yourselves for a little while until his wrath has passed by. 21 See, the LORD is coming out of his dwelling to punish the people of the earth for their sins. The earth will disclose the blood shed upon her; she will conceal her slain no longer. (NIV)

Ark: te-vah': תבה
Tav: sign, mark of covenant. The pictograph is that of a cross.
Bet: house, household, family
Hey: behold, reveal. At the end of a word is can mean what comes from or out of, belonging to

The ark is the house of the mark of the covenant.

E. Both Noah and Yeshua brought salvation to mankind. Noah saved mankind in his generation. If he hadn't been righteous, God would have destroyed the whole world. God was "grieved" that He had created man.

> Ge 6:6 The LORD was grieved that he had made man on the earth, and his heart was filled with pain. (NIV)

> Ge 6:13 So God said to Noah, "I am going to put an end to all people, for the earth is filled with violence because of them. I am surely going to destroy both them and the earth.

> Ge 6:18 But I will establish my covenant with you, and you will enter the ark-- you and your sons and your wife and your sons' wives with you. (NIV)

Yeshua is the savior of the world.

> Joh 4:42 They said to the woman, "We no longer believe just because of what you said; now we have heard for ourselves, and we know that this man really is the Savior of the world." (NIV)

1Jo 4:14 And we have seen and testify that the Father has sent his Son to be the Savior of the world. (NIV)

F. Peter says that Noah and his family were saved through water and compares this to baptism.

1Pe 3:20 Who disobeyed long ago when God waited patiently in the days of Noah while the ark was being built. In it only a few people, eight in all, were saved through water, 21 and this water symbolizes baptism that now saves you also-- not the removal of dirt from the body but the pledge of a good conscience toward God. It saves you by the resurrection of Jesus Christ, (NIV)

The ark came out of water and landed on Nisan 17.

Ge 8:4 and on the seventeenth day of the seventh month the ark came to rest on the mountains of Ararat. (NIV)

The nation of Israel was also saved through water on or near Nisan 17. The Passover lamb was slain on Nisan 14 and some days later, the children of Israel crossed the Red Sea.

Ex 14:21 Then Moses stretched out his hand over the sea, and all that night the LORD drove the sea back with a strong east wind and turned it into dry land. The waters were divided, 22 and the Israelites went through the sea on dry ground, with a wall of water on their right and on their left. (NIV)

Yeshua, who rose from the dead on Nisan 17, offers us salvation through "water."

Ac 2:38 Peter replied, "Repent and be baptized, every one of you, in the name of Jesus Christ for the forgiveness of your sins. And you will receive the gift of the Holy Spirit. 39 The promise is for you and your children and for all who are far off—for all whom the Lord our God will call." (NIV)

The second coming will be purification through fire. Two things cleanse: water and fire.

Nu 31:22 Gold, silver, bronze, iron, tin, lead 23 and anything else that can withstand fire must be put through the fire, and then it will be clean. But it must also be purified with the water of cleansing. And whatever cannot withstand fire must be put through that water. (NIV)

Peter tells us that in the time of Noah, the waters were the agent of both judgment and salvation. 1 Peter 3:20-21 which we just read tells us that Noah and his family were saved through water. At the same time, the water of the flood destroyed the wicked. We read further that on the coming Day of Judgment, destruction of the ungodly will come by fire.

> 2Pe 3:6 By these waters also the world of that time was deluged and destroyed. 7 By the same word the present heavens and earth are reserved for fire, being kept for the day of judgment and destruction of ungodly men. (NIV)

Malachi tells us that the fire, like the water, is also the agent of purification. He compares the fire with soap, that is cleansing by water.

> Mal 3:2 But who can endure the day of his coming? Who can stand when he appears? For he will be like a refiner's fire or a launderer's soap. 3 He will sit as a refiner and purifier of silver; he will purify the Levites and refine them like gold and silver. Then the LORD will have men who will bring offerings in righteousness, 4 and the offerings of Judah and Jerusalem will be acceptable to the LORD, as in days gone by, as in former years. (NIV)

> Mal 4:1 "Surely the day is coming; it will burn like a furnace. All the arrogant and every evildoer will be stubble, and that day that is coming will set them on fire," says the LORD Almighty. "Not a root or a branch will be left to them. 2 But for you who revere my name, the sun of righteousness will rise with healing in its wings. And you will go out and leap like calves released from the stall. 3 Then you will trample down the wicked; they will be ashes under the soles of your feet on the day when I do these things," says the LORD Almighty. (NIV)

But like in the time of Noah, after the judgment will come a new beginning.

> 2Pe 3:11 Since everything will be destroyed in this way, what kind of people ought you to be? You ought to live holy and godly lives 12 as you look forward to the day of God and speed its coming. That day will bring about the destruction of the heavens by fire, and the elements will melt in the heat. 13 But in keeping with his promise we are looking forward to a new heaven and a new earth, the home of righteousness. (NIV)

Student Notes for In the Time of Noah: Noah as a type of Messiah

A. Name

    1. Noah's name is also a title for Messiah. (Ge 5:29)

    2. The comforter is a title for the Messiah. (Mat 11:29, Joh 14:16)

Hebrew word picture: Hebrew is read right to left.

Noah: No-ach': נח

Noon: נ life

Chet: ח The eighth letter. It begins a new cycle of seven, and thus stands for new beginnings.

Noah is the beginning of new life.

Comforter: me-nach-em: מנחם

Mem: מ Water

No-ach: נח a quiet peace

Mem: ם Water

*The mem is written as ם at the end of a word and מ everywhere else in a word.

The comforter is a quiet peace in the midst of the waters.

B. Righteousness

    1. Noah was righteous (Ge 6:9, Heb 11:7)

    2. Yeshua was righteous. (Heb 1:8, 2Pe 1:1)

C. Preacher of righteousness
    1. Noah preached righteousness. (2Pe 2:5)

    2. Yeshua preached righteousness. (Mat 4:17, Isa 51:8, 1Pe 3:18-20a)

D. World ignored preaching about coming judgment
    1. In Noah's time (Ge 6:11, Mat 24:38-39)

    2. Israel, as a nation, rejected Yeshua (Ac 2:23, Is 53:3, Ps 118:22)

    3. When Yeshua comes again (2Pe 3:5, Re 3:3, Lu 17:26-28, Lu 17:34-37)

Taken: 3880. παραλαμβνω paralambano, par-al-am-ban'-o from 3844 and 2983; to receive near

Left: 863. αφιημι aphiemi, af-ee'-ay-mee to send forth

Where will they be sent? (Rev 19:17-18, 21, Mat 13:30)

In what other way is Yeshua's second coming like the time of the flood? (Ge 8:7-9, Job 1:7, 1Pe 5:8)

A raven, like an eagle or a vulture is a _____

The dove continued to return to the ark until it found a green olive branch. (Ge 8:10-12)

Noah stayed in the ark until judgment was complete. (Is 26:20-21)

Ark: te-vah': תבה

Tav: ת sign, mark of covenant. The pictograph is that of a cross.

Bet: ב house, household, family

Hey: ה behold, reveal. At the end of a word the "hey" can mean what comes from or out of, belonging to

The ark is the house of the mark of the covenant.

E. Savior of the world.
　　1. Noah saved mankind. (Ge 6:6, Ge 6:13, 18)

　　2. Yeshua is the savior of the world. (Joh 4:42, 1Jo 4:14)

F. Saved through water.

      1. Noah and his family were saved out of the water. (1Pe 3:20-21, Ge 8:4)

      2. Nation of Israel was saved through water (Ex 14:21-22)

      3. Yeshua, who rose from the dead, offers us salvation through "water."
(Ac 2:38-39)

      4. Second coming will be salvation through fire.
Two things cleanse: (Nu 31:22-23, 2 Pe 3:6-7, Mal 3:2-4, Mal 4:1-3, 2 Pe 3:11-13)

Discussion Questions for In the Time of Noah

1. Noah's parents said Noah would comfort them concerning their toil because God cursed the land. How does this refer to the promise of a redeemer to Adam and Eve? (Ge 3:17-19)

2. Contrast the righteousness of Noah with the actions of the rest of his generation. How did Yeshua characterize His generation? (Lu 11:29-32)

3. How are the times of Noah, Yeshua, and the second coming all alike? Describe most people's level of concern as the time of Yeshua's second coming approaches.

4. Peter writes of both the judgment and salvation by water in the time of Noah. How can water be both judgment and salvation? Malachi writes that in the latter days judgment and purification both come by fire. Discuss how this is both similar to and different than by water.

5. Luke 17:34-37 is used to support the doctrine that a rapture occurs that takes the saved and leaves behind the unsaved to face a later judgment. The Greek words in this passage indicate one group is received near and the other group sent away. Read Matthew 7:21-23, Matthew 13:24-30, 36-43, 47-50, Matthew 25:14-30.
A. Do these passages support the idea of the unjust being left behind to face a later judgment or being sent away?

B. How do these passages speak of resurrection and judgment?

"To Your seed, I will give this land" Genesis 12:7

God promised blessings to Abraham because he heard and obeyed God's voice. One of the promises was that the land would belong to Abraham's seed. The word "seed" in this verse is singular, so the land will go to a specific descendant of Abraham.

A. The book of Galatians identifies this seed: The land belongs to Yeshua.

> Ga 3:16 The promises were spoken to Abraham and to his seed. The Scripture does not say "and to seeds," meaning many people, but "and to your seed," {verse 16 quotes Gen. 12:7; 13:15; 24:7} meaning one person, who is Christ. (NIV)

B. The land was so important to God, that the Israelites were to observe a Sabbath for the land every seventh year. They were not to plow or plant but to live off of the fruit that occurred naturally from the land and from the abundance of the previous year. If they were faithful to follow His decrees, the land would produce abundantly especially in the sixth year before the Sabbatical year.

> Le 25:1 The LORD said to Moses on Mount Sinai, 2 "Speak to the Israelites and say to them: when you enter the land I am going to give you, the land itself must observe a sabbath to the LORD. 3 For six years sow your fields, and for six years prune your vineyards and gather their crops. 4 But in the seventh year the land is to have a sabbath of rest, a sabbath to the LORD. Do not sow your fields or prune your vineyards. 5 Do not reap what grows of itself or harvest the grapes of your untended vines. The land is to have a year of rest. 6 Whatever the land yields during the sabbath year will be food for you-- for yourself, your manservant and maidservant, and the hired worker and temporary resident who live among you, 7 as well as for your livestock and the wild animals in your land. Whatever the land produces may be eaten. (NIV)

> Le 25:18 "'Follow my decrees and be careful to obey my laws, and you will live safely in the land. 19 Then the land will yield its fruit, and you will eat your fill and live there in safety. 20 You may ask, "What will we eat in the seventh year if we do not plant or harvest our crops?" 21 I will send you such a blessing in the sixth year that the land will yield enough for three years. (NIV)

This is a remembrance of the Garden of Eden before the fall. As a result of Adam's sin, man would have to toil to raise food implying that before the fall, Adam didn't have to toil.

> Ge 3:19 By the sweat of your brow you will eat your food until you return to the ground, since from it you were taken; for dust you are and to dust you will return." (NIV)

It is a foreshadowing of the messianic reign of Christ. When Yeshua reigns with righteousness and judgment the land will produce abundantly.

Eze 34:24 I the LORD will be their God, and my servant David will be prince among them. I the LORD have spoken. 25 "'I will make a covenant of peace with them and rid the land of wild beasts so that they may live in the desert and sleep in the forests in safety. 26 I will bless them and the places surrounding my hill. I will send down showers in season; there will be showers of blessing. 27 The trees of the field will yield their fruit and the ground will yield its crops; the people will be secure in their land. They will know that I am the LORD, when I break the bars of their yoke and rescue them from the hands of those who enslaved them. (NIV)

But Israel did not keep the Sabbatical years. God sent judgment to Israel through Assyria and Babylon. Assyria carried off the ten northern tribes of Israel, and Babylon carried off Judah and Benjamin. Judah's period of captivity was the number of Sabbaths for the land that they failed to observe.

2Ch 36:20 He carried into exile to Babylon the remnant, who escaped from the sword, and they became servants to him and his sons until the kingdom of Persia came to power. 21 The land enjoyed its sabbath rests; all the time of its desolation it rested, until the seventy years were completed in fulfillment of the word of the LORD spoken by Jeremiah. (NIV)

C. When the Israelites took possession of the land, they were not to sell the land permanently because it belonged to God through His son Yeshua.

Le 25:23 "The land must not be sold permanently, because the land is mine and you are but aliens and my tenants. 24 Throughout the country that you hold as a possession, you must provide for the redemption of the land." (NIV)

In the year of Jubilee which came every 50 years, the land was to revert to its original family.

Le 25:8 "'Count off seven sabbaths of years-- seven times seven years-- so that the seven sabbaths of years amount to a period of forty-nine years. 9 Then have the trumpet sounded everywhere on the tenth day of the seventh month; on the Day of Atonement sound the trumpet throughout your land. 10 Consecrate the fiftieth year and proclaim liberty throughout the land to all its inhabitants. It shall be a jubilee for you; each one of you is to return to his family property and each to his own clan. (NIV)

The land could be redeemed early by any kinsman willing to purchase back the land for a price compatible with the number of years left until the next Jubilee. This is what happened in the book of Ruth. Boaz is the kinsman of Naomi's husband, Elimilech. He purchases back the land that Naomi's husband had to sell during the time of famine.

Ru 4:9 Then Boaz said to the elders and all the people, "You are witnesses today that I have bought from the hand of Naomi all that belonged to Elimelech and all that belonged to Chilion and Mahlon. 10 "Moreover, I have acquired Ruth the Moabitess, the widow of Mahlon, to be my wife in order to raise up the name of the deceased on his inheritance, so that the name of the deceased will not be cut off from his brothers or from the court of his birth place; you are witnesses today." (NAS)

Hebrew word picture: Hebrew is read right to left

Redeemer: ga-el': גאל

Gimel: ג camel, to lift up

Aleph-lamed: אל El a name of God

Redeemer is God lifted up.

God: El: אל

Aleph: א ox, strength, first

Lamed: ל staff, shepherd, leader, authority, voice

God is the first voice, the strong authority.

In the word picture, we see that the redeemer is God lifted up. When we lift God in praise, He comes in all His glory. When Solomon dedicated the temple to God, the trumpeters and singers praised God with one voice and His glory filled the temple.

> 2 Chr 5:13 indeed it came to pass, when the trumpeters and singers were as one, to make one sound to be heard in praising and thanking the LORD, and when they **lifted up their voice** with the trumpets and cymbals and instruments of music, and praised the LORD, saying: "For He is good, For His mercy endures forever," that the house, the house of the LORD, was filled with a cloud, (NKJV)

In another sense of lifted up, when Yeshua was lifted up on the cross to die for our sins, He became our redeemer paying the price to buy us back from slavery to sin and death.

> Joh 12:32 "And I, if I am lifted up from the earth, will draw all peoples to Myself." 33 This He said, signifying by what death He would die. (NKJV)

Jeremiah writes of God the Redeemer of Israel bringing rest to the land after the exile to Babylon when He brings Israel and Judah home.

> Jer 50:33 Thus says the LORD of hosts: "The children of Israel were oppressed, Along with the children of Judah; All who took them captive have held them fast; They have refused to let them go. 34 Their Redeemer is strong; The LORD of hosts is His name. He will thoroughly plead their case, That He may give rest to the land, And disquiet the inhabitants of Babylon. (NKJV)

Even though God used Assyria and Babylon to deliver His judgment on Israel and Judah, He in turn brings judgment on Assyria and Babylon for being the agent of that very judgment! God always brings judgment on those who oppress Israel!

In Joel, God says that He is bringing judgment upon the nations because they 1) "scattered my people" and 2) "divided up my land."

> Joe 3:1 'In those days and at that time, when I restore the fortunes of Judah and Jerusalem, 2 I will gather all nations and bring them down to the Valley of Jehoshaphat. {2 Jehoshaphat means the LORD judges} There I will enter into judgment against them concerning my inheritance, my people Israel, for they scattered my people among the nations and divided up my land. (NIV)

Ezekiel prophesies to the mountains of Israel about judgment to come to the nations 3) due to their possession of the mountains of Israel.

> Eze 36:1 "Son of man, prophesy to the mountains of Israel and say, 'O mountains of Israel, hear the word of the LORD. 2 This is what the Sovereign LORD says: The enemy said of you, "Aha! The ancient heights have become our possession," 5 this is what the Sovereign LORD says: In my burning zeal I have spoken against the rest of the nations, and against all Edom, for with glee and with malice in their hearts they made my land their own possession so that they might plunder its pastureland.' 7Therefore this is what the Sovereign LORD says: I swear with uplifted hand that the nations around you will also suffer scorn. 8 "'But you, O mountains of Israel, will produce branches and fruit for my people Israel, for they will soon come home. (NIV)

Even now, the nations around Israel are trying to divide up her land. The heart of the so-called "disputed land" is the very mountains of Israel written about in this passage. Any land Israel has given up in her quest for peace with the Arabs and to appease the critical nations of the world has reverted to its desolate state.

D. From the time of the Assyrian exile, when Israel was taken captive (2 Kings 17:6, 23), no year of Jubilee for the land was possible. The twelve tribes were not in the land! God will gather the people of Israel and return them to the land.

> Eze 28:25 "'This is what the Sovereign LORD says: When I gather the people of Israel from the nations where they have been scattered, I will show myself holy among them in the sight of the nations. Then they will live in their own land, which I gave to my servant Jacob. (NIV)

God Himself has already set the boundaries of Israel. He will prevail.

> Eze 47:13 This is what the Sovereign LORD says: "These are the boundaries by which you are to divide the land for an inheritance among the twelve tribes of Israel, with two portions for Joseph. 14 You are to divide it equally among them.

Because I swore with uplifted hand to give it to your forefathers, this land will become your inheritance. (NIV)

The year of Jubilee, when the land is restored to its original family is heralded by the sound of the shofar and a proclamation of liberty to both the 1) people and 2) land.

Le 25:9 'Then you shall cause the trumpet of the Jubilee to sound on the tenth day of the seventh month; on the Day of Atonement you shall make the trumpet to sound throughout all your land. 10 'And you shall consecrate the fiftieth year, and proclaim liberty throughout all the land to all its inhabitants. It shall be a Jubilee for you; and each of you shall return to his possession, and each of you shall return to his family. (NKJV)

Isaiah speaks of the day when liberty is proclaimed. It is "the acceptable year of the LORD and the day of vengeance of our God."

Isa 61:1 "The Spirit of the Lord GOD is upon Me, Because the LORD has anointed Me To preach good tidings to the poor; He has sent Me to heal the brokenhearted, To proclaim liberty to the captives, And the opening of the prison to those who are bound; 2 To proclaim the **acceptable year of the LORD, And the day of vengeance of our God**; To comfort all who mourn, 3 To console those who mourn in Zion, To give them beauty for ashes, The oil of joy for mourning, The garment of praise for the spirit of heaviness; That they may be called trees of righteousness, The planting of the LORD, that He may be glorified." (NKJV)

Yeshua quoted the first part of this passage when He began His ministry. He declared the acceptable year of the LORD but not the day of vengeance.

Lu 4:16 He went to Nazareth, where he had been brought up, and on the Sabbath day he went into the synagogue, as was his custom. And he stood up to read. 17 The scroll of the prophet Isaiah was handed to him. Unrolling it, he found the place where it is written: 18 "The Spirit of the Lord is on me, because he has anointed me to preach good news to the poor. He has sent me to proclaim freedom for the prisoners and recovery of sight for the blind, to release the oppressed, 19 to proclaim the year of the Lord's favor." 20 Then he rolled up the scroll, gave it back to the attendant and sat down. The eyes of everyone in the synagogue were fastened on him, 21 and he began by saying to them, "Today this scripture is fulfilled in your hearing." (NIV)

When John the Baptist was in prison, he sent some of his followers to Yeshua to ask if he was the Messiah. Yeshua replied that they should report what they had seen.

Lu 7:22 NKJV 22 Jesus answered and said to them, "Go and tell John the things you have seen and heard: that the blind see, the lame walk, the lepers are cleansed, the deaf hear, the dead are raised, the poor have the gospel preached to them.

Everything they observe fulfills the acceptable year of the Lord, but not the day of vengeance. The second part of this passage will be fulfilled when He returns to bring vengeance.

> Isa 63:1 Who is this coming from Edom, from Bozrah, with his garments stained crimson? Who is this, robed in splendor, striding forward in the greatness of his strength? "It is I, speaking in righteousness, mighty to save." 2 Why are your garments red, like those of one treading the winepress? 3 "I have trodden the winepress alone; from the nations no one was with me. I trampled them in my anger and trod them down in my wrath; their blood spattered my garments, and I stained all my clothing. 4 For the day of vengeance was in my heart, and the year of my redemption has come. (NIV)

E. During the Year of Jubilee, the land was again to observe a Sabbath. During the millennium, God restores the Promised Land.

> Isa 4:2 In that day the Branch of the LORD will be beautiful and glorious, and the fruit of the land will be the pride and glory of the survivors in Israel. (NIV)

Those who mourn will indeed be comforted and receive beauty for ashes. But this is just the beginning! At the end of the millennial reign, the entire creation will be liberated. Paul writes that even now it waits in eager expectation of that redemption.

> Ro 8:19 For the earnest expectation of the creation eagerly waits for the revealing of the sons of God. 20 For the creation was subjected to futility, not willingly, but because of Him who subjected it in hope; 21 because the creation itself also will be delivered from the bondage of corruption into the glorious liberty of the children of God. (NKJV)

When the New Jerusalem comes after the millennial reign, the land will be fully redeemed from the curse it was under due to Adam's sin.

> Ge 3:17 To Adam he said, "Because you listened to your wife and ate from the tree about which I commanded you, 'You must not eat of it,' "Cursed is the ground because of you; through painful toil you will eat of it all the days of your life. (NIV)

The land will no longer be cursed; it will yield its fruit throughout the year nourished by the river of life that flows from the temple.

> Re 22:1 Then the angel showed me the river of the water of life, as clear as crystal, flowing from the throne of God and of the Lamb 2 down the middle of the great street of the city. On each side of the river stood the tree of life, bearing twelve crops of fruit, yielding its fruit every month. And the leaves of the tree are for the healing of the nations. 3 No longer will there be any curse. The throne of God and of the Lamb will be in the city, and his servants will serve him. (NIV)

Student Notes for "To Your seed, I will give this land" Outline Genesis 12:7

God promised blessings to Abraham. One of these is the promise of the land. We will look at who is the heir to the land. When Israel had possession of the land it was to observe a Sabbath. We will see that this is both a remembrance of the Garden of Eden and a foreshadowing of the rule of Yeshua during the millennium and ultimately of the return of the whole earth to the state of a Garden of Eden.

A. Who is the Seed: (Ga 3:16)
      The land belongs to_____

B. The Land was to observe a Sabbath of rest. (Le 25:1-7)
      1. The requirements were:

      2. How would they live without crops? (Le 25:18-21)

      3. Remembrance of the Garden of Eden: (Ge 3:19)

      4. Foreshadow of the reign of Messiah (Eze 34:24-27)

      5. Judah's period of captivity in Babylon: (2Chr 36:20-21)

C. Selling of the land: (Le 25:23-24)

    1. Redemption of the land in the Year of Jubilee: (Le 25:8-10)

    2. Boaz redeemed the land of Elimilech (Ru 4:9-10)

Hebrew word picture: Hebrew is read right to left

Redeemer: ga-el': גאל

Gimel: ג camel, to lift up

Aleph-lamed: אל El a name of God

Redeemer is God lifted up.

God: El: אל

Aleph: א ox, strength, first

Lamed: ל staff, shepherd, leader, authority, voice

God is the first voice, the strong authority.

---

    3. The redeemer is lifted up: (2Chr 5:13, Joh 12:32-33, Jer 50:33-34)

    4. Judgment against the nations: (Joe 3:1-2, Eze 36:1-8)

        1.

        2.

        3.

D. God will gather the people of Israel and return them to the land. (Eze 28:25, Eze 47:13-14)

    1. The year of Jubilee proclaims liberty to: (Le 25:9-10)
        1.

        2.

  2. It is the: (Isa 61:1-3) _____

  3. Yeshua quoted the first part of this passage when He began His ministry. (Lu 4:16-21, Lu 7: 22)

  4. The second part of this passage, "the day of vengeance of our God," will be fulfilled when He returns. (Isa 63:1-4)

E. Fulfillment of the year of Jubilee for the land.
    1. The millennium (Isa 4:2, Ro 8:19-21)

    2. The new heaven and earth (Ge 3:17, Re 22:1-3)

Discussion Questions for "To Your Seed, I will Give the Land"

1. How is the Sabbatical year for the land like the weekly Sabbath for man? (Ex 16:22-26, Ex 20:8-11)

2. What was the curse on the land because of the disobedience of Israel? How is this like the curse on the ground because of Adam's disobedience? (Jer 25:9-12)

3. How is the Jubilee year like a remembrance of the Garden of Eden and a foreshadowing of the millennial reign?

4. Who will the land of Israel belong to in the millennial reign? (Eze 47:13- 48:35)

5. One of the eternal promises of the covenant is that God will give Israel the Promised Land. What are some other promises of the Covenant?

6. Not only is the land of Israel God's inheritance, but so are the people of Israel. (Joe 3:12) How do these go hand in hand?

The Kingdom of Heaven Suffers Violence?

A. The passage in Matthew 11:10-15, contains a baffling sentence. Yeshua is discussing who John the Baptist is and that, even as great as he is, anyone in the kingdom of heaven is greater than he. He goes on to describe the kingdom of heaven in verse 12. In the New International Version Yeshua says, "… the kingdom of God has been forcefully advancing and forceful men lay hold of it." The New King James version renders it, "And from the days of John the Baptist until now the kingdom of heaven suffers violence, and the violent take it by force." The whole passage reads as follows in the Modern King James Version.

> Mat 11:10 For this is the one of whom it is written, "Behold, I send My messenger before Your face, who shall prepare Your way before You." 11 Truly I say to you, Among those who have been born of women there has not risen a greater one than John the Baptist. But the least in the kingdom of Heaven is greater than he. 12 And from the days of John the Baptist until now the kingdom of Heaven is taken by violence, and the violent take it by force. 13 For all the prophets and the law prophesied until John. 14 And if you will receive it, this is Elijah who is to come. 15 He who has ears to hear, let him hear. (MKJV)

How can the kingdom of heaven be taken by force? How can violent men take the kingdom of God? This doesn't seem to make sense, so we need to dig deeper into the verse. We look at the meanings of the Greek words used to get a better understanding of this passage. Then we look for other scriptures to explain this scripture. Is there a similar passage in the Tanakh or Old Testament that sheds light on this passage? Yeshua's teachings were always grounded in the Tanakh.

First, let's look at the Greek words behind our English to get a deeper understanding of the connotations of these phrases and words. The Greek words translated to the phrases "taken by violence" and "violent" both come from the Greek word "bios" #979 through the idea of vital activity; force, violence. Bio, of course, means life. The phrase "take by force" is from the word "harpazo" #726 meaning to seize, to catch away, to pluck, pull, take (by force).

Taken by violence: #971 biazo: from #979: to force, to crowd oneself (into) or (passively) to be seized, press, suffer violence.

Violent: #973 biastes: from #971; a forcer, energetic, violent.

#979: βιοϖ bios, a primary word; life, i.e. (literally) the present state of existence; by implication, the means of livelihood:--good, life, living.

Take by force: #726 harpazo: #726 meaning to seize, to catch away, to pluck, pull, take (by force).

Finally, the book of Luke has a companion passage to our passage in Matthew but in condensed form.

> Lu 16:16 "The Law and the Prophets were proclaimed until John. Since that time, the good news of the kingdom of God is being preached, and everyone is forcing his way into it." (NIV)

Luke equates Matthew's expression "taking the kingdom of God by force" with forcing one's way into the kingdom. But how do you force your way into the kingdom of God or take it by force? There are three points in these passages:

1. John the Baptist prepares the way for the Messiah. In Matthew 11:11, Yeshua is quoting a verse from Malachi.

> Mal 3:1 NKJV 1 "Behold, I send My messenger, And he will prepare the way before Me. And the Lord, whom you seek, Will suddenly come to His temple, Even the Messenger of the covenant, In whom you delight. Behold, He is coming," Says the LORD of hosts.

2. The Kingdom of God is being preached.
3. There is a force, violence or vital activity associated with it.

The sages pair Malachi 3:1 about preparing the way of the Messiah with a similar verse in Micah 2:12-13. Both are about someone going ahead of others.

> Mic 2:12 "I will surely gather all of you, O Jacob; I will surely bring together the remnant of Israel. I will bring them together like sheep in a pen, like a flock in its pasture; the place will throng with people. 13 One who breaks open the way will go up before them; they will break through the gate and go out. Their king will pass through before them, the LORD at their head." (NIV)

In Hebraic thought, when two verses or passages are linked, referring to one passage automatically refers to the other as well. So, when Yeshua refers to the passage in Malachi, the passage in Micah is also called to mind. The passage in Micah is similar to our passage in Matthew about the kingdom of heaven suffering violence and the violent taking it by force. Like Matthew, Micah talks about one who breaks open the way and others who break open the gate. Both contain the image of throngs of people. So examining the passage in Micah will shed light on the passage in Matthew.

In Micah 2:13, the phrase "one who breaks open" is actually one word, Strong's #6555 paratz meaning to break or burst out. It is also a proper name, Peretz, meaning to breach or break forth. The first part of Micah 2:13, then reads, "Peretz will go up before them; they will break (paratz) through the gate and go out." Peretz leads the way out of the sheepfold, breaking through the gate. The typical sheepfold had walls made of rocks with a gap left for a doorway. At night, the shepherd would bring the sheep into the fold, and then sleep in the entryway. This prevented the sheep from leaving and the predators from getting in. In the morning, the sheep were eager to get out and would crowd around the doorway. The shepherd went out first, and then the sheep pushed their way through the doorway. The concluding sentence in verse 13 tells us that it is Messiah who leads the way.

In the language of Micah, Matthew 11:12 reads, "From the time of John the Baptist until now, the kingdom of heaven is breaking out, and the breaker is breaking out." Or perhaps, "… the kingdom of heaven is bursting forth and the energetic press into it."

We read in Mark 1:15, that at this same time, when Herod put John the Baptist in prison, Yeshua was proclaiming:

> Mar 1:15 and saying, "The time is fulfilled, and the kingdom of God is at hand. Repent, and believe in the gospel." (NKJV)

The word time is (#2540) kairos actually meaning a set time. The time Yeshua is talking about was set or already determined and it is now at hand, right next to them, within touching distance. Matthew says that the Law (Torah) and all the prophets right up until John prophesied about this set time. The kingdom of God is happening right now; it is bursting forth! We can see that Yeshua is talking about the explosive growth of the kingdom of God and the enthusiasm of the people to enter it.

John the Baptist prepared the way and Yeshua is present right then and there to **lead** the way. His short ministry on earth has begun. Very soon after this event, He will go to the cross to die for us. But He doesn't stay in the grave; He bursts forth into new life becoming the firstfruits of many brethren.

> Col 1:18 And he is the head of the body, the church; he is the beginning and the firstborn from among the dead, so that in everything he might have the supremacy. (NIV)

> 1Co 15:20 But Christ has indeed been raised from the dead, the firstfruits of those who have fallen asleep. (NIV)

Yeshua is there in the entrance to the sheepfold. When the time was right, He led the way. He showed us the kingdom of heaven on earth and leads the way into eternal life.

B. We seem to have explained the passage in Matthew now, but who is the Peretz that Micah refers to? Examining the identity of Peretz will further enlighten our passage in Matthew. Paretz is spelled Pharez in the KJV and Perez in other versions. Peretz was one of the twin sons of Judah.

> Ge 38:27 When the time came for her (Tamar) to give birth, there were twin boys in her womb. 28 As she was giving birth, one of them put out his hand; so the midwife took a scarlet thread and tied it on his wrist and said, "This one came out first." 29 But when he drew back his hand, his brother came out, and she said, "So this is how you have broken out!" And he was named Peretz. 30 Then his brother, who had the scarlet thread on his wrist, came out and he was given the name Zerah. (NIV)

We see in Peretz a type of Messiah. Peretz is the first to burst forth from the womb; Messiah is the first to burst forth from the grave becoming the firstborn from the dead. Remember the phrases "suffer violence" and "violent" are related to bio through the idea of vital activity; force, violence. Birth is certainly a vital activity with a sort of violence involved.

Peretz is an ancestor of Nahshon, the prince of the tribe of Judah during the Exodus.

> 1Chr 2:5 The sons of Pharez; Hezron, and Hamul. 9 The sons also of Hezron, that were born unto him; Jerahmeel, and Ram, and Chelubai. 10 And Ram begat Amminadab; and Amminadab begat Nahshon, prince of the children of Judah; (KJV)

> Nu 2:3 And those that encamp on the east side toward the sunrising shall be they of the standard of the camp of Judah, according to their hosts: and the prince of the children of Judah shall be Nahshon the son of Amminadab. (ASV)

> Nu 10:14 The divisions of the camp of Judah went first, under their standard. Nahshon son of Amminadab was in command. (NIV)

Like Peretz before him and Yeshua after him, Nahshon led the way with the entire camp of Israelites following. Tradition also says that it was Nahshon who was the first to step into the Red Sea. His sister was Elisheva, the wife of Aaron. (Ex. 6:23). Nahshon was the first to offer sacrifices after the dedication of the tabernacle (Num. 7:12). Nahshon leads the way through "baptism" in the Red Sea. He is at their head as they march from Mt. Sinai up to Kadish Barnea where they were to enter the Promised Land. Unfortunately, the rebellion caused by the bad report of the ten spies kept them out of the Promised Land at that time. Similarly, the lack of faith of some of the Jewish people during Yeshua's time, kept them from entering the spiritual Promised Land as well.

Peretz leads the way out of the womb into life. Yeshua leads the way as the captain of the Lord of Hosts, as the first to die and rise again becoming the firstfruits of the resurrection. But Isaiah 52:12 says that when the LORD leads the Israelites back to Israel, He will go before and behind them.

> Isa 52:9 Burst into songs of joy together, you ruins of Jerusalem, for the LORD has comforted his people, he has redeemed Jerusalem. 10 The LORD will lay bare his holy arm in the sight of all the nations, and all the ends of the earth will see the salvation of our God. 11 Depart, depart, go out from there! Touch no unclean thing! Come out from it and be pure, you who carry the vessels of the LORD. 12 But you will not leave in haste or go in flight; for the LORD will go before you, the God of Israel will be your rear guard. (NIV)

Peretz led the way. Who followed Peretz out of the womb? Who is the rear guard?

Ge 38:30 Afterward his brother came out who had the scarlet thread on his hand. And his name was called Zerah. (NKJV)

Peretz's brother, Zerah, followed him out of the womb. The name Zerah is from #2226 meaning a rising of light, to irradiate or shoot forth beams, to rise (as the sun), to appear. Yeshua's second coming is compared to the rising of the sun.

Isa 60:1 "Arise, shine, for your light has come, and the glory of the LORD rises upon you. 2 See, darkness covers the earth and thick darkness is over the peoples, but the LORD rises upon you and his glory appears over you. 3 Nations will come to your light, and kings to the brightness of your dawn. (NIV)

Mal 4:2 But for you who revere my name, the sun of righteousness will rise with healing in its wings. And you will go out and leap like calves released from the stall. (NIV)

Peretz foreshadows the first coming of Yeshua who led the way, bursting forth from the grave to bring new life to all who believe in Him. Zerah foreshadows His second coming. The promised Messiah son of David couldn't come until Messiah son of Joseph first came to suffer and die breaking the bonds of death and bringing salvation to the world. So, Zerah pulled back his hand allowing Peretz to be born first. Now the way is clear for Zerah to be born, for the Messiah son of David to finally come and establish His kingdom forever.

C. Peretz is also an ancestor of Boaz who in turn is an ancestor of David. Ruth 4:18 starts the listing of the "generations" of Peretz which culminates in David.

Ru 4:18 Now these are the generations of Pharez: Pharez begat Hezron, 19 And Hezron begat Ram, and Ram begat Amminadab, 20 And Amminadab begat Nahshon, and Nahshon begat Salmon, 21 And Salmon begat Boaz, and Boaz begat Obed, 22 And Obed begat Jesse, and Jesse begat David. (KJV)

The word for "generations" in the phrase "these are the generations" is #8435 toledot. This phrase or the phrase "the book of the generations" is used eleven times in Genesis, once in Numbers, once in Ruth, and once in Matthew, but the spelling is not always the same. The first use of the phrase is in Genesis 2:4 before the fall of Adam when sin entered the world.

Ge 2:4 These are the generations of the heavens and of the earth when they were created, in the day that the LORD God made the earth and the heavens, (KJV)

Toledot is spelled, from right to left תּוֹלְדוֹת. In the next use of the phrase listing the generations of Adam, toledot is spelled תּוֹלְדֹת with the second וֹ, (vav) missing. It is spelled with one vav missing right up until the generations of Peretz listed in Ruth.

The explanation for the different spellings is that before sin entered the world, the generations were complete and whole. After the fall, the generations of creation were diminished and would not be restored until the Son of Peretz comes and restores all things.

The Bible contains the phrase "these are the generations" eleven times with the defective spelling. Eleven is the number of defect, disorder or imperfection. The use of the phrase eleven times emphasizes the imperfection of the generations following Adam until the promise of the Son of Peretz who breaks out, opening the way into the kingdom of heaven. Peretz's generations culminate in David, and Yeshua, of course, is referred to as the "Son of David." The phrase "these are the generations" is used three times with the full spelling concluding with the phrase "these are the generations" in reference to Yeshua's genealogy in the original Hebrew manuscripts of Matthew chapter 1. The number three represents divine completion. With the coming of Yeshua, God's divine plan for the restoration of mankind is nearing completion. When Yeshua comes again, the plan will be finished.

Paul speaks in Romans about creation being subject to sin and liberated when Yeshua comes again.

> Ro 8:20 For the creation was subjected to frustration, not by its own choice, but by the will of the one who subjected it, in hope 21 that the creation itself will be liberated from its bondage to decay and brought into the glorious freedom of the children of God. 22 We know that the whole creation has been groaning as in the pains of childbirth right up to the present time. (NIV)

John writes of the removal of the curse when the New Jerusalem descends from heaven.

> Re 22:1 Then the angel showed me the river of the water of life, as clear as crystal, flowing from the throne of God and of the Lamb 2 down the middle of the great street of the city. On each side of the river stood the tree of life, bearing twelve crops of fruit, yielding its fruit every month. And the leaves of the tree are for the healing of the nations. 3 No longer will there be any curse. The throne of God and of the Lamb will be in the city, and his servants will serve him. (NIV)

D. The picture language for toledot, תולדות is also enlightening. In the picture language, we see that the sign of the covenant brackets the shepherd leading the way through the doorway. But in the diminished spelling, the second vav is missing. As a result, the covenant is disconnected from the doorway. The pathway has been blocked off just like the way back to the Garden of Eden was blocked. But Yeshua restores the connections; He makes the generations complete and the way is open once again.

Hebrew word picture: Hebrew is read right to left

Generations: toledot, תולדות

Tav, ת cross, seal or covenant

Vav, ו nail, peg, connect or attach

Lamed, ל shepherd's staff, authority, leader

The Dalet, ד door, doorway, pathway, entrance

Vav, ו nail, peg, connect or attach

Tav, ת cross, seal or covenant

The generations are the sign of the covenant surrounding the shepherd leading the way through the doorway.

In Genesis 5, when the vav is first missing, there are ten generations listed from Adam to Noah. The passage in Ruth that has the restored vav also lists ten generations. Ten is the number of a completed cycle or the entirety of the matter. It is the number of the divine perfection of order. Other examples of the number ten are the number of righteous men required in order to spare Sodom and Gomorrah, the number of the plagues on Egypt, and the number of the summarized commandments of God.

The meanings of the names in the ten generations from Adam to Noah tell the gospel story from the fall of man to the coming of Yeshua and his death on the cross. The vav is missing, man has fallen and only God can redeem Him. (A full listing of the names with their full meanings is in lesson one of this volume. Here, we include a condensed list.)

Adam: mankind
Seth: is appointed to
Enos: feeble, frail mortality
Cainan: a fixed dwelling place
Mahaleel: God who is praised
Jared: descends, comes down
Enoch: to instruct, train up
Methuselah: a man sent forth
Lamech: to be beaten, smitten, tortured
Noah: comfort, quiet peace

The generations read, "Mankind is appointed to feeble, frail mortality, a fixed dwelling place. God who is praised comes down to instruct as a man sent forth to be beaten, smitten, tortured bringing comfort, a quiet peace."

The meanings of the names in the ten generations from Peretz to David pick up with the resurrection of Yeshua bursting forth from the grave leading us into His kingdom elaborating on the words from Micah. The vav is restored, God has redeemed man; Yeshua is coming to reign on His eternal throne.

Peretz: #6556 פרץ perets, peh'-rets from 6555; a break (literally or figuratively):-- breach, breaking forth

Hezron: #2696. חצרון Chetsrown, khets-rone' from 2691; court-yard;
> #2691. a yard (as enclosed by a fence); also a hamlet (as similarly surrounded with walls)

Ram: #7410. רם active participle of 7311; high, from #7311 a primitive root; to be high actively, to rise or raise bring up, exalt

Aminidab: #5992. עמינדב `Ammiynadab, am-mee-naw-dawb' from 5971 and 5068; people of liberality:
> #5068. נדב nadab, naw-dab' a primitive root; to impel; hence, to volunteer (as a soldier), to present spontaneously:--offer freely

Nahshon: #5177. נחשון Nachshown, nakh-shone'; whisperer, enchanter from #5172
> #5172: to prognosticate: predict from the signs (Dictionary.com definition for prognosticate)

Salmon: #8012. שלמון Salmown, sal-mone' from 8008; investiture
> #8008: a dress, clothes, garment, raiment

Boaz: with strength (According to Jewish Encyclopedia)

Obed: 05744. עובד `Owbed, o-bade' active participle of 5647; serving
> #5647: to work, bondsmen, servant, worshipper

Jesse: #3448. ישי Yishay, yee-shah'-ee from the same as 3426
> #3426: exist; entity; used adverbially or as a copula for the substantive verb, there is or are, or any other form of the verb to be

David: #1732. דוד David, daw-veed'; from the same as 1730; loving
> #1730: to love; by implication, a love- token, lover, friend; (well-) beloved

The generations of Peretz read, "One who breaks out of the walled courtyard, high and exalted, (with) a people impelled, a people who offer themselves freely, (to) the one who whispers, who is predicted from the signs. (They are) invested with garments of strength, servants and worshippers, existing to be beloved."

Mic 2:13 One who breaks open the way will go up before them; they will break through the gate and go out. Their king will pass through before them, the LORD at their head." (NIV)

With the ten generations of Ruth, we see a completed cycle culminating in David, a man after God's own heart leading us into eternal life.

In Matthew, the generations of Yeshua aren't listed in sets of ten but in three sets of fourteen.

Mat 1:17 So all the generations from Abraham to David are fourteen generations. And from David until the carrying away into Babylon, fourteen generations. And from the carrying away into Babylon until Christ, fourteen generations. (MKJV)

The number of David's name is 14. David: דוד: 4+6+4=14. Refer to Appendix A: The Hebrew Alphabet to see how the letters are also numbers.

Yeshua is the divine completion of David's line. His generations are calling out, "David, David, David!"

Isa 9:7 Of the increase of His government and peace There will be no end, Upon the throne of David and over His kingdom, To order it and establish it with judgment and justice From that time forward, even forever. The zeal of the LORD of hosts will perform this. (NKJV)

Student Notes for The Kingdom of Heaven Suffers Violence?

A. Yeshua describes the coming of the kingdom of Heaven in confusing language:

Mat 11:10 For this is the one of whom it is written, "Behold, I send My messenger before Your face, who shall prepare Your way before You." 11 Truly I say to you, Among those who have been born of women there has not risen a greater one than John the Baptist. But the least in the kingdom of Heaven is greater than he. 12 And from the days of John the Baptist until now the kingdom of Heaven is taken by violence, and the violent take it by force. 13 For all the prophets and the law prophesied until John. 14 And if you will receive it, this is Elijah who is to come. 15 He who has ears to hear, let him hear. (MKJV)

Vocabulary:
Taken by violence: #971 biazo: from #979: to force, to crowd oneself (into) or (passively) to be seized, press, suffer violence.

Violent: #973 biastes: from #971; a forcer, energetic, violent.

#979: βιοω bios, a primary word; life, i.e. (literally) the present state of existence; by implication, the means of livelihood:--good, life, living.

Take by force: #726 harpazo: #726 meaning to seize, to catch away, to pluck, pull, take (by force).

A. But, how do you force your way into the kingdom of God or take it by force?
   (Lu 16:16)
There are three points in these passages:
   1. (Mal 3:1)

   2.

   3.

Micah writes about one who will "break open" the way and leads the way. (Mic 2:12-13)

Vocabulary: One who breaks open: #6555 paratz: To break or burst out

A rephrase of Mat 11:12: From the time of John the Baptist until now, _____

_____

The Kingdom of Heaven (Mar 1:15)

John _____, Yeshua _____ (Col 1:18, 1Co 15:20)

B. Who is Peretz? (Ge 38:27-30)
1. Son of _____

2. First to _____

3. An ancestor of (1Chr 2:5, 9-10)_____

    a. Led the way (Nu 2:3, Nu 10:14

    b. Aaron's brother-in-law

    c. First to offer the sacrifices of dedication

Yeshua leads the way (Isa 52:9-12)

Who came after Peretz? (Ge 38:30)

Zerah #2226: from #2226 meaning a rising of light, to irradiate or shoot forth beams, to rise (as the sun), to appear.

Yeshua's' second coming compared to (Isa 60:1-3, Mal 4:2) _____

C. Peretz begins the listing of the generations that culminate in David (Ru 4:18-22)

Generations: #8435 toledot

1. Usual spelling תולדת

Spelling in Ru 4:18 and Ge 2:4 תולדות

2. Before the fall

_____,

after the fall

_____

Eleven times with the defective spelling:

Three times with the full spelling:

Creation will be liberated when Yeshua comes again (Ro 8:20-22, Re 22:1-3)

D. Picture language for generations, toledot:

> Hebrew word picture: Hebrew is read right to left
>
> Generations: toledot, תולדות
>
> Tav, ת cross, seal or covenant
>
> Vav, ו nail, peg, connect or attach
>
> Lamed, ל shepherd's staff, authority, leader
>
> The Dalet, ד door, doorway, pathway, entrance
>
> Vav, ו nail, peg, connect or attach
>
> Tav, ת cross, seal or covenant
>
> The generations are the sign of the covenant surrounding the shepherd leading the way through the doorway.

Ten generations from Adam to Noah:

Ten generations from Peretz to David:

Peretz: #6556 פרץ perets, peh'-rets from 6555; a break (literally or figuratively):-- breach, breaking forth

Hezron: #2696. חצרון Chetsrown, khets-rone' from 2691; court-yard;
> #2691. a yard (as inclosed by a fence); also a hamlet (as similarly surrounded with walls)

Ram: #7410. רם active participle of 7311; high, from #7311 a primitive root; to be high actively, to rise or raise bring up, exalt

Aminidab: #5992. עמינדב `Ammiynadab, am-mee-naw-dawb' from 5971 and 5068; people of liberality:
> #5068. נדב nadab, naw-dab' a primitive root; to impel; hence, to volunteer (as a soldier), to present spontaneously:--offer freely

Nahshon: #5177. נחשון Nachshown, nakh-shone'; whisperer, enchanter from #5172
#5172: to prognosticate: predict from the signs (Dictionary.com definition for prognosticate)

Salmon: #8012. שלמון Salmown, sal-mone' from 8008; investiture
#8008: a dress, clothes, garment, raiment

Boaz: with strength (According to Jewish Encyclopedia)

Obed: 05744. עובד `Owbed, o-bade' active participle of 5647; serving
#5647: to work, bondsmen, servant, worshipper

Jesse: #3448. ישי Yishay, yee-shah'-ee from the same as 3426
#3426: exist; entity; used adverbially or as a copula for the substantive verb, there is or are, or any other form of the verb to be

David: #1732. דוד David, daw-veed' from the same as 1730; loving
#1730: to love; by implication, a love- token, lover, friend; (well-) beloved

The generations of Peretz read, "One who breaks out of the walled courtyard, high and exalted, (with) a people impelled, a people who offer themselves freely, (to) the one who whispers, who is predicted from the signs. (They are) invested with garments of strength, servants and worshippers, existing to be beloved."

> Mic 2:13 One who breaks open the way will go up before them; they will break through the gate and go out. Their king will pass through before them, the LORD at their head." (NIV)

The generations of Yeshua: (Mat 1:17, Isa 9:7)

Discussion Questions for the Kingdom of God Suffers Violence?

1. Yeshua said in John 3:3-7 that we must be born again. How is this like breaking out into the kingdom of Heaven?

2. Yeshua proclaimed in Mark 1:15 that the kingdom of God is at hand. He then continued with the instructions to repent and believe the gospel. The word gospel is from the Greek meaning good news. Read Isaiah 52:7-8 about good news. How is this like the breaking out into the kingdom of Heaven that Yeshua describes?

3. In Joshua 5:13-15, the Captain of the LORD of Hosts appears before the battle at Jericho, the first battle to take the Promised Land. How is this like Yeshua's second coming bursting into the kingdom?

4. We are currently in the sheepfold of our physical lives. Yeshua breaks the way into eternal life. How does the restoration of the letter ו, vav, in the word toledot (generations) illustrate this concept?

5. Read John 5:25-30 and John 10:24-28. How does this fit in with the image of the shepherd and the sheep bursting out of the sheepfold?

6. Yeshua's second coming also liberates creation itself. How is this a breaking out? (Read also Matthew 24:7-8)

Why Moses Couldn't Go Into the Promised Land

Just before the Israelites were to go into the land after 40 years in the wilderness, the Israelites complained that they had no water. God's instructions to Moses and Aaron were that they were to speak to the rock and the rock would provide water.

> Nu 20:8 "Take the rod; you and your brother Aaron gather the congregation together. Speak to the rock before their eyes, and it will yield its water; thus you shall bring water for them out of the rock, and give drink to the congregation and their animals." (NKJV)

Moses and Aaron followed God's instructions except Moses struck the rock twice instead of speaking to the rock. As a result, God said that neither Aaron nor Moses would go into the Promised Land.

> Nu 20:9 So Moses took the rod from before the LORD as He commanded him. 10 And Moses and Aaron gathered the assembly together before the rock; and he said to them, "Hear now, you rebels! Must we bring water for you out of this rock?" 11 Then Moses lifted his hand and struck the rock twice with his rod; and water came out abundantly, and the congregation and their animals drank. 12 Then the LORD spoke to Moses and Aaron, "Because you did not believe Me, to hallow Me in the eyes of the children of Israel, therefore you shall not bring this assembly into the land which I have given them." (NKJV)

A. In what way did Moses fail to believe and hallow God? Moses believed that the rock would bring forth water. It seems like Moses just got a little more forceful and dramatic than God instructed. Examining some of the words in their original Hebrew will shed some light on this issue. In verse 8, God tells Moses to gather the congregation. The word God uses for congregation is 'edah.

Congregation: #5712. עדה 'edah, ay-daw' feminine of 5707 in the original sense of fixture; a stated assemblage (specifically, a concourse, or generally, a family or crowd):-- assembly, company, congregation, multitude, people, swarm. Compare with 5713

#5707 עד 'ed, ayd contracted from 5749 ; concretely, a witness; abstractly, testimony; specifically, a recorder, i.e. prince:--witness.

#5713 עדה 'edah, ay-daw' feminine of 5707 in its techn. sense; testimony:-- testimony, witness. Compare 5712.

Notice the Hebrew edah can be either congregation #5712 or witness #5713. When a word can take on more than one meaning, in scriptures it usually takes on both, one in the literal sense of the passage and one in a more symbolic sense. In this case, we have added meaning to the passage when we consider both meanings of the word edah. God told Moses to call the congregation as witnesses.

> Hebrew word picture: Hebrew reads right to left.
>
> Witness: ayd: עד
>
> Ayin: ע eye, to see
>
> Dalet: ד Door, pathway
>
> Witness is to see the door or pathway.
>
> Testimony: ay-daw:
>
> Ayin: ע eye, to see
>
> Dalet: ד Door, pathway
>
> Hey: ה Behold, reveal, at the end of a word it means what comes from or belonging to
>
> Testimony is what comes from seeing the pathway.

In verse 10, Moses gathers the congregation, but the word Moses uses is kahal.

Congregation: #6950 קהל qahal, 'kaw-hal' a primitive root; to convoke:--assemble (selves) (together), gather (selves) (together).

Moses merely gathered the congregation disregarding the choice of the congregation as witnesses. He goes further and calls the congregation rebels instead of witnesses! Moses seems to have lost his love for his people. In contrast, when the Israelites built the Golden Calf, Moses interceded on their behalf.

> Ex 32:11 Then Moses pleaded with the LORD his God, and said: "LORD, why does Your wrath burn hot against Your people whom You have brought out of the land of Egypt with great power and with a mighty hand? 12 "Why should the Egyptians speak, and say, 'He brought them out to harm them, to kill them in the mountains, and to consume them from the face of the earth'? Turn from Your fierce wrath, and relent from this harm to Your people. 13 "Remember Abraham, Isaac, and Israel, Your servants, to whom You swore by Your own self, and said to them, 'I will multiply your descendants as the stars of heaven; and all this land that I have spoken of I give to your descendants, and they shall inherit it forever.'" (NKJV)

They were God's people not rebels! Also, Moses shows some arrogance. According to Moses, "we" are going to bring water from the rock. At the best, Moses is referring to himself and God. At the worst, he is referring to himself and Aaron leaving God out altogether.

Two questions come to mind about God's choice of the word 'edah for congregation. The first is what were the people to witness? They had already seen God bring water from a rock when they were first brought out of Egypt. This was not a new event. Those who were children at the time would remember this event. The others would certainly have been told about it. The second is where had they been getting water all these years? Let's address the second question first.

B. Where did they get water for forty years in the wilderness? God brought water from the rock at Rephidim shortly after He delivered them from Egypt.

> Ex 17:5 And the LORD said to Moses, "Go on before the people, and take with you some of the elders of Israel. Also take in your hand your rod with which you struck the river, and go. 6 "Behold, I will stand before you there on the rock in Horeb; and you shall strike the rock, and water will come out of it, that the people may drink." And Moses did so in the sight of the elders of Israel. 7 So he called the name of the place Massah and Meribah, because of the contention of the children of Israel, and because they tempted the LORD, saying, "Is the LORD among us or not?" (NKJV)

But where did they get water the rest of the forty years in the wilderness? There were between two and a half and three million people who left Egypt in addition to all their livestock. Exodus tells us that six hundred thousand men of Israel went up from Egypt.

> Ex 12:37 Then the children of Israel journeyed from Rameses to Succoth, about six hundred thousand men on foot, besides children. 38 A mixed multitude went up with them also, and flocks and herds-a great deal of livestock. (NKJV)

If a wife and two children accompanied each man, there were 2.4 million Israelites who left Egypt. Then there were the "mixed multitude" of Egyptians who accompanied them along with all their livestock. If we say 2.5 million people and allow 1 quart of water for each person each day, they would need 625,000 gallons of water per day just for the drinking water for the people!

Nothing short of God could provide that much water. Paul alludes to the source of water in his letter to the Corinthians.

> 1Co 10:1 Moreover, brethren, I do not want you to be unaware that all our fathers were under the cloud, all passed through the sea, 2 all were baptized into Moses in the cloud and in the sea, 3 all ate the same spiritual food, 4 and all drank the same spiritual drink. For they drank of that spiritual Rock that followed them, and that Rock was Christ. (NKJV)

We can see that this refers to the Exodus. They all crossed the Red Sea being symbolically baptized with water. The cloud of God's presence was with them each day. Manna was provided for their food, referred to here as "spiritual food." They all drank of the water from the rock here referred to, like the manna, as "spiritual drink." The following chart summarizes Paul's analogy.

Verse	Physical	Spiritual
1	Crossed the Red Sea	Baptized with water
2	Cloud of God's presence	Received the Holy Spirit
3	Ate Manna	Ate of the Bread of Life
4	Drank water from the rock	Drank of living water

What was the source of water? The rock followed them! The Jewish sages in a commentary on Numbers 20 say that "this water-giving rock miraculously accompanied the Children of Israel throughout their wanderings in the desert." Paul, who was educated under the great teacher Gamaliel would be familiar with this teaching.

> Ac 22:3 "I am a Jew, born in Tarsus of Cilicia, but brought up in this city. Under Gamaliel I was thoroughly trained in the law of our fathers and was just as zealous for God as any of you are today. (NIV)

When the water first came from the rock at Rephidim, the place was called Massah and Meribah. The water from the rock in Numbers 20 is called the "water of Meribah" associating this water with the water from the original rock.

> Ex 17:7 So he called the name of the place Massah and Meribah, because of the contention of the children of Israel, and because they tempted the LORD, saying, "Is the LORD among us or not?" (NKJV)

> Nu 20:13 This was the water of Meribah, because the children of Israel contended with the LORD, and He was hallowed among them. (NKJV)

We can see the meanings of Massah and Meribah when we compare different translations of Psalm 95:8. The meaning of Massah is testing and the meaning of Meribah is rebellion or provocation.

> Ps 95:8 "Do not harden your hearts, as in the **rebellion**, As in the day of **trial** in the wilderness, (NKJV)
> Ps 95:8 do not harden your hearts as you did at **Meribah**, as you did that day at **Massah** in the desert, (NIV)

If the rock was the source of the water all those years, why did it cease to give water at that time? What happened at the time the water dried up?

> Nu 20:1 Then the children of Israel, the whole congregation, came into the Wilderness of Zin in the first month, and the people stayed in Kadesh; and Miriam died there and was buried there. 2 Now there was no water for the congregation; so they gathered together against Moses and Aaron. (NKJV)

Miriam died! Symbolically, Miriam, Aaron and Moses represented the three offices of Messiah. Moses was the leader representing Yeshua's office as king. Although Moses acted as prophet and priest, his primary role was as the leader. Aaron was the priest representing Yeshua's office of priest. Miriam was a prophetess representing Yeshua's office as prophet.

> Ex 15:20 Then Miriam the prophetess, the sister of Aaron, took the timbrel in her hand; and all the women went out after her with timbrels and with dances. (NKJV)

God's words through the prophet Micah say that He sent Moses, Aaron, and Miriam as leaders before the Israelites.

> Mic 6:4 For I brought thee up out of the land of Egypt, and redeemed thee out of the house of servants; and I sent before thee Moses, Aaron, and Miriam. (KJV)

In Yeshua's first coming, his role was that of prophet calling the people to repentance.

> Lu 5:32 "I have not come to call the righteous, but sinners, to repentance." (NKJV)

> Lu 24:46 Then He said to them, "Thus it is written, and thus it was necessary for the Christ to suffer and to rise from the dead the third day, 47 "and that repentance and remission of sins should be preached in His name to all nations, beginning at Jerusalem. (NKJV)

Hebrew word picture:

Miriam: Mir-yam:

Yood-Reysch-Mem: מרי Mer-ee': bitter, bitterness

Mem: ם Water

Miriam is bitter water. Yeshua drank of the "bitter water" and then died.

At His death, his physical incarnation as prophet ended. He spent three days and nights in the grave. The source of water was cut off! As priest, He offered up Himself as the perfect sacrifice for sin. He continues to act as our priest even now making intercession for us.

> Ro 8:34 Who is he who condemns? It is Christ who died, and furthermore is also risen, who is even at the right hand of God, who also makes intercession for us.(NKJV)

> Heb 7:25 Therefore He is also able to save to the uttermost those who come to God through Him, since He always lives to make intercession for them. 26 For such a High Priest was fitting for us, who is holy, harmless, undefiled, separate from sinners, and has become higher than the heavens; 27 who does not need daily, as those high priests, to offer up sacrifices, first for His own sins and then for the people's, for this He did once for all when He offered up Himself. 28 For the law appoints as high priests men who have weakness, but the word of the oath, which

came after the law, appoints the Son who has been perfected forever. 8:1 Now this is the main point of the things we are saying: We have such a High Priest, who is seated at the right hand of the throne of the Majesty in the heavens, (NKJV)

When He comes again, He will come primarily as the ruling king but He will take on all the offices. Zechariah speaks of Him as priest and king. Micah says that He will teach us the Word. After all, He is the Living Word! Thus, He is prophet, priest and king.

Zec 6:11 "Take the silver and gold, make an elaborate crown, and set it on the head of Joshua the son of Jehozadak, the high priest. 12 "Then speak to him, saying, 'Thus says the LORD of hosts, saying: "Behold, the Man whose name is the BRANCH! From His place He shall branch out, And He shall build the temple of the LORD; 13 Yes, He shall build the temple of the LORD. He shall bear the glory, And shall sit and rule on His throne; So He shall be a priest on His throne, And the counsel of peace shall be between them both."' (NKJV)

Mic 4:2 Many nations shall come and say, "Come, and let us go up to the mountain of the LORD, To the house of the God of Jacob; He will teach us His ways, And we shall walk in His paths." For out of Zion the law shall go forth, And the word of the LORD from Jerusalem. (NKJV)

This answers the question of where they got water in wilderness. They got it from the rock which represents Yeshua. Then, when Miriam died, the water ceased to flow representing the death of Yeshua the prophet.

C. This leads us to the first of our questions. What was the congregation to witness? They were to witness the "resurrection" of the rock. Paul said that the spiritual rock from which they drank was Christ. (1Cor. 10:4). Rock is a title of Messiah in many places. There are so many places where He is referred to as Rock that they cannot even begin to be covered in this short lesson. The first place is when Jacob is blessing his sons. Of Joseph, who is a type of Messiah, Jacob says,

Ge 49:24 But his bow remained steady, his strong arms stayed limber, because of the hand of the Mighty One of Jacob, because of the Shepherd, the Rock of Israel, (NIV)

Messiah is referred to as the Rock five times in the Song of Moses (Deuteronomy 32:4-31) and five times in David's first Psalm written at his victory over the Philistines (2 Samuel 22:2-51). The number five is the number of grace. There are five books of Torah. Deuteronomy, the fifth book, is the book of grace. The fifth kingdom in Daniel's vision is the kingdom of Messiah. Psalm 95, which contains the reference to Massah and Meribah, starts by calling the Messiah the Rock of our Salvation.

Ps 95:1 Oh come, let us sing to the LORD! Let us shout joyfully to the Rock of our salvation. (NKJV)

Jeremiah speaks of water that comes from a rock as part of a parable about the stubbornness of Israel.

> Jer 18:11 "Now therefore, speak to the men of Judah and to the inhabitants of Jerusalem, saying, 'Thus says the LORD: "Behold, I am fashioning a disaster and devising a plan against you. Return now every one from his evil way, and make your ways and your doings good."'" 12 And they said, "That is hopeless! So we will walk according to our own plans, and we will every one obey the dictates of his evil heart."

> 13 Therefore thus says the LORD: "Ask now among the Gentiles, Who has heard such things? The virgin of Israel has done a very horrible thing. 14 **Will a man leave the snow water of Lebanon, Which comes from the rock of the field?** Will the cold flowing waters be forsaken for strange waters? 15 "Because My people have forgotten Me, They have burned incense to worthless idols. And they have caused themselves to stumble in their ways, From the ancient paths, To walk in pathways and not on a highway, (NKJV)

This gives new meaning to Yeshua's words when teaching during the Feast of Tabernacles.

> Joh 7:37 On the last and greatest day of the Feast, Yeshua stood and said in a loud voice, "If anyone is thirsty, let him come to me and drink. (NIV)

Yeshua is indeed the Rock providing the life giving water. Without the water in the wilderness, the Israelites would have died.

Now, let's look at Moses' instructions again. He was supposed to take the rod. Which rod?

> Nu 20:8 "Take the rod; you and your brother Aaron gather the congregation together. Speak to the rock before their eyes, and it will yield its water; thus you shall bring water for them out of the rock, and give drink to the congregation and their animals." (NKJV)

The first time the water came from the rock, the rod Moses used was Aaron's rod.

> Ex 17:5 And the LORD said to Moses, "Go on before the people, and take with you some of the elders of Israel. Also take in your hand **your rod with which you struck the river**, and go. (NKJV)

> Ex 7:19 Then the LORD spoke to Moses, "**Say to Aaron, 'Take your rod** and stretch out your hand over the waters of Egypt, over their streams, over their rivers, over their ponds, and over all their pools of water, that they may become blood. And there shall be blood throughout all the land of Egypt, both in buckets of wood and pitchers of stone.'" 20 And Moses and Aaron did so, just as the LORD commanded. **So he lifted up the rod and struck the waters** that were in the river,

in the sight of Pharaoh and in the sight of his servants. And all the waters that were in the river were turned to blood. (NKJV)

The rod was Aaron's rod. What was special about Aaron's rod? Aaron's rod had budded as a sign that God had chosen only Aaron's line as priests. A rod is a dead stick but Aaron's rod budded and produced almonds. (Num. 17:1-8) The almond tree is the first to bloom in the spring reinforcing the image of new life. The Hebrew for almond tree is shaw-kade', שקד. The Hebrew for watch is shaw-kad' שקד. The only difference is the vowel markings. Again, we have the image of watching for new life. This rod had been placed in front of the Testimony, the Ark of the Covenant, as a sign to the rebellious.

> Nu 17:10 And the LORD said to Moses, "Bring Aaron's rod back before the Testimony, to be kept as a sign against the rebels, that you may put their complaints away from Me, lest they die." (NKJV)

This is the rod that was used. The "living" rod!

Why was it important that Moses speak to the rock? The Rock that was Christ was to be smitten only once for the sins of man.

> Heb 7:26 For such a High Priest was fitting for us, who is holy, harmless, undefiled, separate from sinners, and has become higher than the heavens; 27 who does not need daily, as those high priests, to offer up sacrifices, first for His own sins and then for the people's, for this He did **once for all** when He offered up Himself. (NKJV)

> Heb 10:12 But this Man, after He had offered one sacrifice for sins forever, sat down at the right hand of God, (NKJV)

> Isa 53:5 But He was wounded for our transgressions, He was bruised for our iniquities; The chastisement for our peace was upon Him, And by His stripes we are healed. (NKJV)

What was the timing of this event? It happened in the first month, the same month in which Passover occurs.

> Nu 20:1 Then the children of Israel, the whole congregation, came into the Wilderness of Zin in the first month, and the people stayed in Kadesh; and Miriam died there and was buried there. (NKJV)

The sages say that Miriam died on Nisan 10, the day that the Passover lambs were brought into Jerusalem. Moses and Aaron would be in mourning for her for seven days. Further, if either of them had been in the tent when Miriam died or had come into contact with her body, they would be unclean for seven days (Num. 19:11) Moses would be unable to approach God about the water for seven days. It also explains Moses' impatience with the Israelites; his sister had just died and the Israelites wouldn't leave him alone! It would be seven days later on Nisan 17, before Moses could approach God, get instructions for providing water and acting on them. Nisan 17 is also the Feast of Firstfruits of the barley harvest and the day that Yeshua the Messiah would rise from the grave some 1500 years later.

Why couldn't Moses go into the Promised Land? God answered in Numbers 20:12, "Because you did not believe Me, to hallow Me in the eyes of the children of Israel, therefore you shall not bring this assembly into the land which I have given them." The witnesses were gathered to see God's resurrection power and a powerful picture of the resurrection of Messiah the source of living water and Moses failed to convey that meaning.

D. Imagine the event as it should have happened. Moses, acting in his role of prophet, priest and king, holding up the living rod, the tree of life, speaking to the Rock, Yeshua the Messiah, out of which will flow rivers of living water. What words would he have used? We can only imagine.

Let us say with David, "He is the Rock of our salvation." With joy, let us draw water from the wells of salvation.

> 2Sa 22:47 "The LORD lives! Blessed be my Rock! Let God be exalted, The Rock of my salvation! (NKJV)

> Isa 12:3 Therefore with joy you will draw water from the wells of salvation. (NKJV)

> Joh 4:13 Jesus answered and said to her, "Whoever drinks of this water will thirst again, 14 "but whoever drinks of the water that I shall give him will never thirst. But the water that I shall give him will become in him a fountain of water springing up into everlasting life." (NKJV)

> Re 22:1 And he showed me a pure river of water of life, clear as crystal, proceeding from the throne of God and of the Lamb. 2 In the middle of its street, and on either side of the river, was the tree of life, which bore twelve fruits, each tree yielding its fruit every month. The leaves of the tree were for the healing of the nations. (NKJV)

> Zec 14:8 And in that day it shall be That living waters shall flow from Jerusalem, Half of them toward the eastern sea And half of them toward the western sea; In both summer and winter it shall occur. (NKJV)

126

Student Notes for Why Moses Couldn't Go Into the Promised Land

Just before the Israelites were to go into the land after 40 years in the wilderness, the Israelites complained that they had no water. God's instructions to Moses and Aaron were that they were to speak to the rock and the rock would provide water.

A. Striking instead of speaking (Nu 20:8-12)

1. Congregation (refer to Nu 20:8):

Congregation: #5712. עדה `edah, ay-daw' feminine of 5707 in the original sense of fixture; a stated assemblage (specifically, a concourse, or generally, a family or crowd):--assembly, company, congregation. Compare with 5713

#5707 עד `ed, ayd contracted from 5749 ; concretely, a witness; abstractly, testimony; specifically, a recorder, i.e. prince:--witness.

#5713 עדה `edah, ay-daw' feminine of 5707 in its techn. sense; testimony:--testimony, witness. Compare 5712.

Hebrew word picture: Hebrew reads right to left.

Witness: ayd: עד

Ayin: ע eye, to see

Dalet: ד Door, pathway

Witness is to see the door or pathway.

Testimony: ay-daw: עדה

Ayin: ע eye, to see

Dalet: ד Door, pathway

Hey: ה Behold, reveal, at the end of a word it means what comes from or belonging to

Testimony is what comes from seeing the pathway.

---

2. Congregation (refer to Nu 20:10)

Congregation: #6950 קהל qahal, 'kaw-hal' a primitive root; to convoke:--assemble (selves) (together), gather (selves) (together).

3. Moses' love for his people (Ex 32:11-13, refer to Nu 20:10)

B. Where did they get water for forty years in the wilderness? (Ex 17:5-7)

1. At least 2.5 million people (Ex 12:37-38)

2. Paul describes the source: (1Co 10:1-4)

Verse	Physical	Spiritual
1		
2		
3		
4		

3. The sages say: (Ac 22:3)

4. When the water first came from the rock at Rephidim, the place was called Massah and Meribah. (Ex 17:7, Nu 20:13, Ps95:8 compare NKJV, NIV)

Massah:

Meribah:

5. If the rock was the source of the water all those years, why did it cease to give water at that time? (Nu 20:1-2)

a. The Prophetess/ Prophet (Ex 15:20, Mic 6:4, Lu 5:32, Lu 24:46-47)

> Hebrew word picture:
>
> Miriam: Mir-yam: מרים
>
> Yood-Reysch-Mem: מרי Mer-ee': bitter, bitterness
>
> Mem: ם Water
>
> Miriam is bitter water. Yeshua drank of the "bitter water" and then died.

b. The Priest (Ro 8:34, He 7:25-8:1)

c. The King (Zec 6:11-13, Mic 4:2)

Conclusion: Where did they get the water?

C. What was the congregation to witness?
   1. Who or what is the "Rock?" (Ge 49:24, Ps 95:1, Jer 18:11-15, Joh 7:37)

   2. What rod was Moses to take? (Nu 20:8, Ex. 17:5, Ex 7:19-20)

3. What was special about the rod? (Nu 17:10)

      Almond tree: shaw-kade, שקד

      Watch: shaw-ked', שקד

4. Why was it important that Moses speak to the rock? (Heb 7:26-7, Heb 10:12, Isa 53:5)

5. When did this event happen? (Nu 20:1)

      Jewish tradition:

      Moses and Aaron in mourning and unclean:

Why Couldn't Moses go into the Promised Land?

D. Imagine the event as it should have happened.

Let us say with David, "He is the Rock of our salvation." With joy, let us draw water from the wells of salvation. (2Sa 22:47, Isa 12:3, Joh 4:13-14, Re 22:1-2, Zec 14:8)

Discussion Questions for Why Moses Couldn't Go into the Promised Land

1. God told Moses to gather the congregation to witness the "resurrection" of the rock. What is the role of witnesses in the scriptures? (De 19:15, De 30:19, Jos 24:22, Isa 44:6-9, Ac 10:39-41)

2. Moses used Aaron's rod which was a sign against the rebels. How was Moses a rebel in this situation?

3. How are the manna and the water from the rock a symbol of Yeshua?

4. Discuss "Rock" as a title for Messiah. How is Yeshua the Rock of our salvation?

5. A prophet or prophetess is one who speaks God's words. Miriam is identified as a prophetess at the time of the crossing of the Red Sea. What do we know about her words and actions that could qualify her as a prophetess?

6. One of Yeshua's last miracles was raising Lazarus from the dead. He did so in front of many witnesses. Contrast Yeshua's words in John 11:40-44 with Moses' words in Numbers 20:10-11.

Isaac's Marriage and The Bride of Christ

The marriage of Isaac foreshadows the selection of the bride of Christ and the second coming. The marriage happened after Abraham offered up Isaac as a sacrifice to the LORD.

A. Isaac was probably not a young boy at the time of the sacrifice.

> Ge 22:5 And Abraham said to his young men (na-ar), "Stay here with the donkey; the lad (na-ar) and I will go yonder and worship, and we will come back to you." (NKJV)

Lad: #5288: נַעַר na`ar, nah'-ar from 5287; (concretely) a boy (as active), from the age of infancy to adolescence; by implication, a servant; also (by interch. of sex), a girl (of similar latitude in age):--babe, boy, child, lad, servant, young (man).

#5287: נָעַר na`ar, naw-ar' a primitive root (probably identical with 5286, through the idea of the rustling of mane, which usually accompanies the lion's roar); to tumble about:--shake (off, out, self), overthrow, toss up and down.

#5286: נָעַר na`ar, naw-ar' a primitive root; to growl:--yell.

As we look at the translation of the word na'ar at various places in the Torah, we see a wide variation in the ages of the people described as na'ar. The scriptures use the word na'ar for Ishmael when Abraham sent him away at the age of at least 16. Judah refers to his brother Benjamin as na'ar when Benjamin is the father of ten sons! Moses calls Joshua na'ar at the camp at Mt. Sinai after Joshua had already led the Israelites in battle against the Amalekites. There is one reference to na'ar as a young child and that is to Moses as na'ar when his sister Miriam places him in the basket in the Nile River at the age of three months. So we can't use the word na'ar to establish Isaac's age.

How can we establish a date for Isaac's age? The Jewish sages reference the next chapter of Genesis where we read of Sarah's death at the age of one hundred twenty seven. They postulate that Sarah died shortly after Abraham offered Isaac. In fact, they say that the offering led to her death. If this is the case, Isaac would have been thirty seven years old at the time of the offering.

The scriptures tell us that Abraham and Isaac went together in one accord adding to the evidence that Isaac was not a young boy. The scripture implies that Isaac was of the same purpose as Abraham.

> Ge 22:6 So Abraham took the wood of the burnt offering and laid it on Isaac his son; and he took the fire in his hand, and a knife, and the two of them went together. 7 But Isaac spoke to Abraham his father and said, "My father!" And he said, "Here I am, my son." Then he said, "Look, the fire and the wood, but where is

the lamb for a burnt offering?" 8 And Abraham said, "My son, God will provide for Himself the lamb for a burnt offering." So the two of them went together. (NKJV)

Isaac had to have consented to the sacrifice just as Yeshua consented.

Joh 10:17 "Therefore My Father loves Me, because I lay down My life that I may take it again. 18 "No one takes it from Me, but I lay it down of Myself. I have power to lay it down, and I have power to take it again. This command I have received from My Father." (NKJV)

If Isaac was thirty seven at this event, then his marriage at the age of forty was three years later.

B. Isaac did not choose his own bride; his father Abraham sent his servant to select the bride.

1. Eliezar was probably Abraham's agent. Eliezar means helper of God. Eliezar, the helper of God was sent out to select a bride and the angel of God prepared the way.

Ge 24:2 So Abraham said to the oldest servant of his house, who ruled over all that he had, "Please, put your hand under my thigh, (NKJV)

Ge 15:2 But Abram said, "O Sovereign LORD, what can you give me since I remain childless and the one who will inherit my estate is Eliezer of Damascus?" 3 And Abram said, "You have given me no children; so a servant in my household will be my heir." (NIV)

#461: אֱלִיעֶזֶר 'Eliy`ezer, el-ee-eh'-zer from #410 and #5828; God of help; Eliezer, It can also be rendered helper of God.

We also see that an angel was sent to prepare the way.

Ge 24:7 "The LORD, the God of heaven, who brought me out of my father's household and my native land and who spoke to me and promised me on oath, saying, 'To your offspring I will give this land'-- he will send his angel before you so that you can get a wife for my son from there. (NIV)

2. God has sent helpers to select the bride of Christ. The word apostle means "sent out." The 12 disciples of Yeshua were first called apostles when they were sent out to the villages and towns of Israel.

Mat 9:37 Then he said to his disciples, "The harvest is plentiful but the workers are few. 38 Ask the Lord of the harvest, therefore, to send out workers into his harvest field." 10:1 He called his twelve disciples to him and gave them authority to drive out evil spirits and to heal every disease and sickness. 2 These are the names of the twelve apostles: first, Simon (who is called Peter) and his brother Andrew; James son of Zebedee, and his brother John; (NIV)

This mission as apostles, "sent ones," is given to all believers in the great commission.

Mat 28:18 Then Jesus came to them and said, "All authority in heaven and on earth has been given to me. 19 Therefore go and make disciples of all nations, baptizing them in the name of the Father and of the Son and of the Holy Spirit, 20 and teaching them to obey everything I have commanded you. And surely I am with you always, to the very end of the age." (NIV)

The Spirit of God goes before the apostles to prepare the way. Only those the father draws or selects will come to Him. The following scriptures are some of the ones in which God says He chooses and draws people to Him.

Jer 31:3 The LORD has appeared of old to me, saying: "Yes, I have loved you with an everlasting love; Therefore with lovingkindness I have drawn you. (NKJV)

Joh 6:44 "No one can come to Me unless the Father who sent Me draws him; and I will raise him up at the last day. (NKJV)

Joh 12:32 "And I, if I am lifted up from the earth, will draw all peoples to Myself." (NKJV)

Eph 1:4 just as He chose us in Him before the foundation of the world, that we should be holy and without blame before Him in love, 5 having predestined us to adoption as sons by Jesus Christ to Himself, according to the good pleasure of His will, (NKJV)

1Th 1:4 …knowing, beloved brethren, your election by God. (NKJV)

Col 3:12 Therefore, as the elect of God, holy and beloved, put on tender mercies, kindness, humility, meekness, longsuffering; (NKJV)

C. The bride was not to be from among the Canaanites.

Ge 24:3 "and I will make you swear by the LORD, the God of heaven and the God of the earth, that you will not take a wife for my son from the daughters of the Canaanites, among whom I dwell; (NKJV)

1. The Canaanite practices were evil in God's eyes including the sacrifice of sons and daughters. The line of Canaan was cursed to be servants to his brothers.

Ge 9:25 Then he said: "Cursed be Canaan; A servant of servants He shall be to his brethren." 26 And he said: "Blessed be the LORD, The God of Shem, And may Canaan be his servant. (NKJV)

Ge 15:15 "Now as for you, you shall go to your fathers in peace; you shall be buried at a good old age. 16 "But in the fourth generation they shall return here, for the iniquity of the Amorites is not yet complete." (NKJV)

The Amorites are one of the tribes of Canaanites. So when God is referring to the sin of the Amorites, He is referring to a tribe of Canaanites.

Ge 10:15 Canaan begot Sidon his firstborn, and Heth; 16 the Jebusite, the **Amorite**, and the Girgashite; 17 the Hivite, the Arkite, and the Sinite; 18 the Arvadite, the Zemarite, and the Hamathite. Afterward the families of the Canaanites were dispersed. (NKJV)

2. When Israel came into the land, they were not to marry Canaanites either. The Canaanites would prove to be a continual stumbling block to Israel constantly introducing idol worship and child sacrifice into the nation.

Ex 34:15 "Be careful not to make a treaty with those who live in the land ; for when they prostitute themselves to their gods and sacrifice to them, they will invite you and you will eat their sacrifices. 16 And when you choose some of their daughters as wives for your sons and those daughters prostitute themselves to their gods, they will lead your sons to do the same. (NIV)

De 7:3 "Nor shall you make marriages with them. You shall not give your daughter to their son, nor take their daughter for your son. 4 "For they will turn your sons away from following Me, to serve other gods; so the anger of the LORD will be aroused against you and destroy you suddenly. 5 "But thus you shall deal with them: you shall destroy their altars, and break down their sacred pillars, and cut down their wooden images, and burn their carved images with fire. 6 "For you are a holy people to the LORD your God; the LORD your God has chosen you to be a people for Himself, a special treasure above all the peoples on the face of the earth. (NKJV)

The Israelites were to be a holy nation (set apart). They could not be holy with the corruption of the Canaanites among them. See also 1 Kings 11:1-6, Jos. 23:12-13, Ez. 5:25-27.

3. We, as believers, are also not to marry unbelievers. Each one of us is not to pollute our own body, which is to be a temple of God, by being joined to an unbeliever—one who walks in darkness and worships idols.

2Co 6:14 Do not be unequally yoked together with unbelievers. For what fellowship has righteousness with lawlessness? And what communion has light with darkness? 15 And what accord has Christ with Belial? Or what part has a believer with an unbeliever? 16 And what agreement has the temple of God with idols? For you are the temple of the living God. As God has said: "I will dwell in them And walk among them. I will be their God, And they shall be My people." 17 Therefore "Come out from among them And be separate, says the Lord. Do not touch what is unclean, And I will receive you." (NKJV)

Paul says that the marriage between two believers is like the marriage between Christ and the church. The bride is to be holy and without blemish. An unbelieving bride cannot be holy and without blemish.

Eph 5:25 Husbands, love your wives, just as Christ also loved the church and gave Himself for her, 26 that He might sanctify and cleanse her with the washing of water by the word, 27 that He might present her to Himself a glorious church, not having spot or wrinkle or any such thing, but that she should be holy and without blemish. (NKJV)

D. Abraham did not choose a bride for Isaac from among his own household. He had a large household and all the males in his household were circumcised following the God of Abraham.

Ge 14:14 Now when Abram heard that his brother was taken captive, he armed his **three hundred and eighteen** trained servants who were born in his own house, and went in pursuit as far as Dan. (NKJV)

Ge 17:10 "This is My covenant which you shall keep, between Me and you and your descendants after you: Every male child among you shall be circumcised; 11 "and you shall be circumcised in the flesh of your foreskins, and it shall be a sign of the covenant between Me and you. 12 "He who is eight days old among you shall be circumcised, every male child in your generations, he who is born in your house or bought with money from any foreigner who is not your descendant. 13 "He who is born in your house and he who is bought with your money must be circumcised, and My covenant shall be in your flesh for an everlasting covenant. (NKJV)

Ge 17:23 So Abraham took Ishmael his son, all who were born in his house and all who were bought with his money, every male among the men of Abraham's house, and circumcised the flesh of their foreskins that very same day, as God had said to him. (NKJV)

E. As we read in Genesis 15:2, none of Abraham's household were blood relatives. All of them had joined his household as he traveled (Genesis 12:5). Although Rebecca was a blood relative of Abraham, his great-niece (Gen. 11:27-29a), her immediate family were idol worshipers. We see that when we read that Rebecca's niece Rachel stole her father Laban's idols.

Ge 31:19 Now Laban had gone to shear his sheep, and Rachel had stolen the household idols that were her father's. (NKJV)

Rebecca most likely was not serving God when she was chosen as the bride of Isaac. We also were chosen to be the bride of Christ before we served God.

> Ro 5:8 But God demonstrates His own love toward us, in that while we were still sinners, Christ died for us. (NKJV)

> Eph 1:4 just as He chose us in Him before the foundation of the world, that we should be holy and without blame before Him in love, 5 having predestined us to adoption as sons by Jesus Christ to Himself, according to the good pleasure of His will, (NKJV)

F. Rebecca had to be willing to leave her family and her gods to join Isaac. On no account was Isaac to go to Rebecca.

> Ge 24:4 "but you shall go to my country and to my family, and take a wife for my son Isaac." 5 And the servant said to him, "Perhaps the woman will not be willing to follow me to this land. Must I take your son back to the land from which you came?" 6 But Abraham said to him, "Beware that you do not take my son back there. (NKJV)

> Ge 24:57 So they said, "We will call the young woman and ask her personally." 58 Then they called Rebekah and said to her, "Will you go with this man?" And she said, "I will go." (NKJV)

Similarly, Israel, when brought out of Egypt, was not to return to Egypt. For all the times Israel rebelled against God in the wilderness, He reserved His greatest anger for when they wanted to select new leaders and return to Egypt. That generation was barred from entering the Promised Land.

> Ex 13:17 Then it came to pass, when Pharaoh had let the people go, that God did not lead them by way of the land of the Philistines, although that was near; for God said, "Lest perhaps the people change their minds when they see war, and return to Egypt." (NKJV)

> De 17:16 "But he shall not multiply horses for himself, nor cause the people to return to Egypt to multiply horses, for the LORD has said to you, 'You shall not return that way again.' (NKJV)

> Nu 14:3 "Why has the LORD brought us to this land to fall by the sword, that our wives and children should become victims? Would it not be better for us to return to Egypt?" 4 So they said to one another, "Let us select a leader and return to Egypt." (NKJV)

> Nu 14:20 Then the LORD said: "I have pardoned, according to your word; 21 "but truly, as I live, all the earth shall be filled with the glory of the LORD- 22 "because all these men who have seen My glory and the signs which I did in Egypt and in the

wilderness, and have put Me to the test now these ten times, and have not heeded My voice, 23 "they certainly shall not see the land of which I swore to their fathers, nor shall any of those who rejected Me see it. (NKJV)

As the bride of Messiah, we, also, are to leave our former lives behind and worship only God.

> Jer 16:19 O LORD, my strength and my fortress, My refuge in the day of affliction, The Gentiles shall come to You From the ends of the earth and say, "Surely our fathers have inherited lies, Worthlessness and unprofitable things." 20 Will a man make gods for himself, Which are not gods? 21 "Therefore behold, I will this once cause them to know, I will cause them to know My hand and My might; And they shall know that My name is the LORD. (NKJV)

Psalms 45 is the coronation psalm. It describes the coronation of Messiah and his wedding. Messiah's bride is to leave her own people and her father's house just like Rebecca did.

> Ps 45:10 Listen, O daughter, Consider and incline your ear; Forget your own people also, and your father's house; 11 So the King will greatly desire your beauty; Because He is your Lord, worship Him. (NKJV)

> 1Pe 1:14 as obedient children, not conforming yourselves to the former lusts, as in your ignorance; 15 but as He who called you is holy, you also be holy in all your conduct, 16 because it is written, "Be holy, for I am holy." (NKJV)

> 2Co 6:17 "Therefore come out from them and be separate, says the Lord. Touch no unclean thing, and I will receive you." {17 Isaiah 52:11; Ezek. 20:34,41} 18 "I will be a Father to you, and you will be my sons and daughters, says the Lord Almighty." {18 2 Samuel 7:14; 7:8} 7:1 Since we have these promises, dear friends, let us purify ourselves from everything that contaminates body and spirit, perfecting holiness out of reverence for God. (NIV)

We see this action in Ruth as she joins herself to the Israelites, Naomi's people.

> Ru 1:16 But Ruth said: "Entreat me not to leave you, Or to turn back from following after you; For wherever you go, I will go; And wherever you lodge, I will lodge; Your people shall be my people, And your God, my God. (NKJV)

Naomi's people did not prosper in Moab when they joined themselves to Moab. Paul says that the Gentiles are grafted into Israel not Israel into the Gentiles.

> Ro 11:17 If some of the branches have been broken off, and you, though a wild olive shoot, have been grafted in among the others and now share in the nourishing sap from the olive root, (NIV)

Remember, Abraham was adamant in insisting that Isaac not go back to the land that Abraham came from.

G. Eliezar offered gifts to Rebecca.

> Ge 24:22 So it was, when the camels had finished drinking, that the man took a golden nose ring weighing half a shekel, and two bracelets for her wrists weighing ten shekels of gold, (NKJV)

> Ge 24:53 Then the servant brought out jewelry of silver, jewelry of gold, and clothing, and gave them to Rebekah. He also gave precious things to her brother and to her mother. (NKJV)

We are given gifts as well. First and foremost is the gift of life.

> Ro 6:23 For the wages of sin is death, but the gift of God is eternal life in Christ Jesus our Lord. (NKJV)

We are also given the Holy Spirit and the gifts of the Spirit.

> Joh 14:16 "And I will pray the Father, and He will give you another Helper, that He may abide with you forever-- 17 "the Spirit of truth, whom the world cannot receive, because it neither sees Him nor knows Him; but you know Him, for He dwells with you and will be in you. (NKJV)

> Joh 16:13 But when he, the Spirit of truth, comes, he will guide you into all truth. He will not speak on his own; he will speak only what he hears, and he will tell you what is yet to come. 14 He will bring glory to me by taking from what is mine and making it known to you. 15 All that belongs to the Father is mine. That is why I said the Spirit will take from what is mine and make it known to you. (NIV)

> Eph 1:3 Praise be to the God and Father of our Lord Jesus Christ, who has blessed us in the heavenly realms with every spiritual blessing in Christ. (NIV)

> Eph 1:6 to the praise of his glorious grace, which he has freely given us in the One he loves. 7 In him we have redemption through his blood, the forgiveness of sins, in accordance with the riches of God's grace 8 that he lavished on us with all wisdom and understanding. (NIV)

> Ac 2:38 Peter replied, "Repent and be baptized, every one of you, in the name of Jesus Christ for the forgiveness of your sins. And you will receive the gift of the Holy Spirit. 39 The promise is for you and your children and for all who are far off-- for all whom the Lord our God will call." (NIV)

H. Isaac is not mentioned again in the scriptures until he is seen at his wedding. Notice that only Abraham is mentioned returning to his young men after Abraham proved himself to God by offering Isaac.

> Ge 22:19 So Abraham returned to his young men, and they rose and went together to Beersheba; and Abraham dwelt at Beersheba. (NKJV)

The next time we see Isaac in the scriptures is when he sees Rebecca by Beer Lahai Roi. Beer Lahai Roi means "the well of the living one who sees me."

> Ge 24:62 Now Isaac came from the way of Beer Lahai Roi, for he dwelt in the South. 63 And Isaac went out to meditate in the field in the evening; and he lifted his eyes and looked, and there, the camels were coming. 64 Then Rebekah lifted her eyes, and when she saw Isaac she dismounted from her camel; 65 for she had said to the servant, "Who is this man walking in the field to meet us?" The servant said, "It is my master." So she took a veil and covered herself. 66 And the servant told Isaac all the things that he had done. (NKJV)

Isaac lifts his eyes and sees Rebecca approaching by the well of the living one who sees me. Yeshua will see us as we shall be. Rebecca lifts her eyes and sees Isaac. We will lift our eyes and see Yeshua.

> 1Jo 3:2 Beloved, now we are children of God; and it has not yet been revealed what we shall be, but we know that when He is revealed, we shall be like Him, for we shall see Him as He is. (NKJV)

Rebecca took a veil and covered herself. We also shall clothe ourselves appropriately with acts of righteousness.

> Re 19:7 "Let us be glad and rejoice and give Him glory, for the marriage of the Lamb has come, and His wife has made herself ready." 8 And to her it was granted to be arrayed in fine linen, clean and bright, for the fine linen is the righteous acts of the saints. (NKJV)

142

Student Notes for Isaac's Marriage and the Bride of Christ

The marriage of Isaac foreshadows the selection of the bride of Christ and the second coming. The marriage happened after Abraham offered up Isaac as a sacrifice to the LORD.

A. Isaac was probably not a young boy at the time of the sacrifice. (Ge 22:5)

Lad: #5288: נער na`ar, nah'-ar from 5287; (concretely) a boy (as active), from the age of infancy to adolescence; by implication, a servant; also (by interch. of sex), a girl (of similar latitude in age):--babe, boy, child, damsel (from the margin), lad, servant, young (man).

#5287: נער na`ar, naw-ar' a primitive root (probably identical with 5286, through the idea of the rustling of mane, which usually accompanies the lion's roar); to tumble about:--shake (off, out, self), overthrow, toss up and down.

#5286: נער na`ar, naw-ar' a primitive root; to growl:--yell.

Isaac had to have consented to the sacrifice just as Yeshua consented. (Ge 22:6-8, Joh 10:17-18)

B. Abraham sent his helper to select the bride.
    1. Eliezar (Ge 24:2, Ge 15:2-3, Ge 24:7)).

    Eliezar: #461. אליעזר 'Eliy`ezer, el-ee-eh'-zer from 410 and 5828; God of help; Eliezer, It can also be rendered helper of God.

    2. God has sent helpers to select the bride of Christ. (Mat 9:37-10:2, Mat 28:18-20)

The mission of apostles the "sent ones":

The mission of the Spirit of God (Jer 31:3, Joh 6:44, Joh 12:32, Eph 1:4-5, 1 Th 1:4, Col 3:12)

C. The bride was not to be from among the Canaanites. (Ge 24:3)

1. The Canaanite practices (Ge 9:25-26, Ge 15:15, Ge 10:15-18)

2. When Israel came into the land, they were not to marry Canaanites either. (Ex 34:15-16, De 7:3-6)

3. We, as believers, are also not to marry unbelievers. (2Co 6:14-17, Eph 5:25-27)

D. The bride was not from among Abraham's own household. (Ge 14:14, Ge 17:10-13, Ge 17:23)

E. The Bride was from an idol worshipping family. (Ge 31:19, Ro 5:8, Eph 1:4-5)

F. Rebecca had to be willing to leave her family and her gods to join Isaac. (Ge 24:4-6, Ge 24:57-58)

    1. Isaac was not to go to Rebecca. (Ex 13:17, De 17:16, Nu 14:3-4, Nu 14:20-23, Jer 16:19-21)

    2. Messiah's bride is to leave her father's gods behind. (Ps 45:10-11, 1Pe 1:14-16, 2Co 6:17-7:1, Ru 1:16, Ro 11:17)

G. Eliezar offered gifts to Rebecca. (Ge 24:22, Ge 24:53, Ro 6:23, Joh 14:16-17, Joh 16:13-15, Eph 1:3, Eph 1:6-8, Ac 2:38-39)

C. Isaac is not mentioned again in the scriptures until he is seen at his wedding. (Ge 22:19, Ge 24:62-66)

Beer Lahai Roi means "the well of the living one who sees me."

    1. Isaac lifts his eyes and sees Rebecca. Rebecca lifts her eyes and sees Isaac. (1 Jo 3:2)

    2. Rebecca took a veil and covered herself. (Re 19:7-8)

Discussion Questions for Isaac's Marriage and The Bride of Christ

1. Discuss the possibility of Isaac being a grown man as opposed to a young boy at the time God told Abraham to bring him as an offering.

2. How are we, like Eliezer, sent ones relying on God to show us our path?

3. God prohibited marriage with the Canaanites largely because their practices such as child sacrifice were an abomination to Him. What practices do you think God would have us avoid today? Support your answer with scripture.

4. Another reason God prohibited marriage with the Canaanites was that they would draw them away from God to worship other gods. Give two instances in scripture when marrying Canaanites drew a person or persons away from God. How does this apply to our marriage choices and other relationships?

5. Rebecca, like the Canaanites, was from an idol worshipping family. How is she different from a possible Canaanite bride?

6. Genesis 24:62-66 describes Isaac's first encounter with his bride. Yeshua tells a parable of a master going on a long journey. After his return, the master asks for an accounting from his servants (Lu 19:11-27). How are these two passages similar?

The Hem of the Garment

A. In Matthew 9:20-22, we read of a woman who is healed by merely touching the hem of Yeshua's garment.

> Mat 9:20 And suddenly, a woman who had a flow of blood for twelve years came from behind and touched the hem of His garment. 21 For she said to herself, "If only I may touch His garment, I shall be made well." 22 But Jesus turned around, and when He saw her He said, "Be of good cheer, daughter; your faith has made you well." And the woman was made well from that hour. (NKJV)

Was there anything special about the "hem" of the garment that she touched? Yeshua said her faith made her well. Exactly what was the faith that she exhibited?

First, let's look at the hem of Yeshua's garment. The Greek word translated here as "hem" is kraspedon which means a fringe or tassel.

Hem: #2899. **kraspedon** kras'-ped-on of uncertain derivation; a margin, i.e. (specially), a fringe or tassel:--border, hem.

Kraspadon is also the Greek translation for the word "tassels" in Numbers 15:38 in the Greek Septuagint version of the Old Testament or Tanakh.

> Nu 15:38 "Speak to the children of Israel: Tell them to make tassels (kraspadon) on the corners of their garments throughout their generations, and to put a blue thread in the tassels of the corners. (NKJV)

The Hebrew word for tassels is tzit-tzit.

Tassel: #6734 ציצת tsiytsith, tsee-tseeth' feminine of #6731; a floral or wing-like projection, i.e. a forelock of hair, a tassel:--fringe, lock.

#6731 ציץ tsiyts, tseets or tsits {tseets}; from #6692; properly, glistening, i.e. a burnished plate; also a flower (as bright-colored); a wing (as gleaming in the air):--blossom, flower, plate, wing.

So, by translating the Greek kraspdon into its Hebrew equivalent tzit-tzit and then into English, we get a better understanding of the verse in Matthew in its original cultural context. A better translation of Matthew 9:20 would be "...touched the tassel of His garment" that is the tzit-tzit. Yeshua wore tassels on his garment!

B. So, the woman touched the tassels or tzit-tzit of Yeshua's garment. But what are the tzit-tzit and how are they worn?

> Nu 15:39 "And you shall have the tassel, that you may look upon it and remember all the commandments of the LORD and do them, and that you may not follow the

harlotry to which your own heart and your own eyes are inclined, 40 "and that you may remember and do all My commandments, and be holy for your God. 41 "I am the LORD your God, who brought you out of the land of Egypt, to be your God: I am the LORD your God." (NKJV)

1. The garment on which the tassels were worn was an over-garment called a tallit. It was comparable to a men's suit jacket in that he would wear it while out of the house and in the house if there were guests. It was a four cornered rectangular garment that draped over the shoulders with the tassels attached on the corners. It came in varying lengths. Yeshua, following the dress of the day and the commandments, would have worn the tallit with the tzit-tzit.

2. The tassels were to have a blue thread in them.

Bue: #8504. תכלת techelet, tek-ay'-leth probably for #7827; the cerulean mussel, i.e. the color (violet) obtained therefrom or stuff dyed therewith:--blue.

This color of blue is used throughout the tabernacle. The curtains that made up the outer wall, the veil separating the Holy Place from the Most Holy Place, and the curtain around the courtyard all contained this blue along with scarlet, purple and linen. Linen was always white.

Ex 26:1 "Moreover you shall make the tabernacle with ten curtains of fine woven linen and blue, purple, and scarlet thread; with artistic designs of cherubim you shall weave them. (NKJV)

Ex 26:4 "And you shall make loops of blue yarn on the edge of the curtain on the selvedge of one set, and likewise you shall do on the outer edge of the other curtain of the second set. (NKJV)

Ex 26:31 "You shall make a veil woven of blue, purple, and scarlet thread, and fine woven linen. It shall be woven with an artistic design of cherubim. 32 "You shall hang it upon the four pillars of acacia wood overlaid with gold. Their hooks shall be gold, upon four sockets of silver. 33 And you shall hang the veil from the clasps. Then you shall bring the ark of the Testimony in there, behind the veil. The veil shall be a divider for you between the holy place and the Most Holy." (NKJV)

Ex 27:16 "For the gate of the court there shall be a screen twenty cubits long, woven of blue, purple, and scarlet thread, and fine woven linen, made by a weaver. It shall have four pillars and four sockets. (NKJV)

The high priest's garments contained the same blue with the robe of the ephod of woven cloth dyed blue.

Ex 28:4 "And these are the garments which they shall make: a breastplate, an ephod, a robe, a skillfully woven tunic, a turban, and a sash. So they shall make holy garments for Aaron your brother and his sons, that he may minister to Me as priest. 5 "They shall take the gold, blue, purple, and scarlet thread, and fine linen, 6 "and they shall make the ephod of gold, blue, purple, and scarlet thread, and fine woven linen, artistically worked. (NKJV)

Ex 28:31 "You shall make the robe of the ephod all of blue. (NKJV)

Ex 39:22 He made the robe of the ephod of woven work, all of blue. (NKJV)

3. The blue came from a particular mollusk found off the coast of Israel in the Mediterranean Sea. The process for extracting the dye and the exact source was lost in 638 A.D. when the Arabs overran Israel cutting off access to the snails. In 1858, the particular snail *Murex trunculus* was identified as a possible source of the dye. Through the description in the Talmud and subsequent archeological evidence, it was confirmed that that was indeed the snail from which the dye was taken. The process to extract the dye was finally reinvented in 1985. The blue dye is now available but still rare and expensive.

4. The blue in the tassels of the garments symbolically connects the wearer with the priesthood. The same blue from the same source is used in the garments of the high priest as well as in the tabernacle. The sons of Aaron are priests to Israel, and all Israel are priests to the nations.

Ex 19:6 'And you shall be to Me a kingdom of priests and a holy nation.' These are the words which you shall speak to the children of Israel." (NKJV)

C. The tabernacle and the garments of the high priest were to be made according to the pattern that God gave Moses and are symbolic of the heavenly tabernacle and our High Priest, Yeshua!

Ex 25:9 "According to all that I show you, that is, the pattern of the tabernacle and the pattern of all its furnishings, just so you shall make it. (NKJV)

Ex 25:40 "And see to it that you make them (the instruments and furnishings) according to the pattern which was shown you on the mountain. (NKJV)

Heb 8:1 Now this is the main point of the things we are saying: We have such a High Priest, who is seated at the right hand of the throne of the Majesty in the heavens, 2 a Minister of the sanctuary and of the true tabernacle which the Lord erected, and not man. 3 For every high priest is appointed to offer both gifts and sacrifices. Therefore it is necessary that this One also have something to offer. 4 For if He were on earth, He would not be a priest, since there are priests who offer the gifts according to the law; 5 who serve the copy and shadow of the heavenly things, as Moses was divinely instructed when he was about to make the tabernacle. For He said, "See that you make all things according to the pattern shown you on the mountain." (NKJV)

Believers who choose to wear the tassels wear them as a visible reminder of our High Priest who even now is seated at the right hand of God. The purpose of the tassels, as stated in verses 39 and 40, is to remember the commands and do them.

> Nu 15:39 "And you shall have the tassel, that you may look upon it and remember all the commandments of the LORD and do them, and that you may not follow the harlotry to which your own heart and your own eyes are inclined, 40 "and that you may remember and do all My commandments, and be holy for your God. (NKJV)

The tassels can also be a reminder to believers to remember God's commands and do them, as well as to live a holy life. The words of Yeshua Himself reinforce this command.

> Joh 14:15 "If you love Me, keep My commandments. (NKJV)

> Joh 14:23 Jesus answered and said to him, "If anyone loves Me, he will keep My word; and My Father will love him, and We will come to him and make Our home with him. (NKJV)

> 1Jo 5:3 For this is the love of God, that we keep His commandments. And His commandments are not burdensome. (NKJV)

Peter, who addresses his letter to all the strangers in the world, reminds us that we are to be holy, that is set apart, to God.

> 1Pe 1:13 Therefore, prepare your minds for action; be self-controlled; set your hope fully on the grace to be given you when Jesus Christ is revealed. 14 As obedient children, do not conform to the evil desires you had when you lived in ignorance. 15 But just as he who called you is holy, so be holy in all you do; 16 for it is written: "Be holy, because I am holy." (NIV)

D. Why is it important that the woman touched the tassel not just the hem or any other part of Yeshua's garment? The answer to this question will show us exactly what faith the woman demonstrated that led to her healing.

A title of Messiah is Sun of Righteousness from Malachi 4:2.

> Mal 4:2 But to you who fear My name The Sun of Righteousness shall arise With healing in His wings; And you shall go out And grow fat like stall-fed calves. (NKJV)

So the Messiah would have the characteristic of "healing in His wings." What are wings? The word for wings is kanaph.

Wings: #3671. כנף kanaph, kaw- from #3670; an edge or extremity; specifically (of a bird or army) a wing, (of a garment or bed-clothing) a flap, (of the earth) a quarter, (of a building) a pinnacle:--+ bird, border, corner, end, feather(-ed), overspreading, X quarters, skirt, X sort, uttermost part, wing((-ed)).

This is the same word used for the phrase "corners of their garments" in the Numbers passage about the tassels, "… they make them fringes (tsiytsith) in the borders (kanaph) of their garments." In Jewish thought the corners of the garments were associated with the tassels and became almost synonymous. So, by touching the tzit-tzit the woman was asserting her faith that Yeshua was the Messiah and thus had healing in His wings—His tzit-tzit.

> Mat 9:21 For she said to herself, "If only I may touch His garment, I shall be made well." (NKJV)

This adds further meaning to Yeshua's statement in verse 22.

> Mat 9:22 But Jesus turned around, and when He saw her He said, "Be of good cheer, daughter; your faith has made you well." And the woman was made well from that hour. (NKJV)

Not only did she have faith that Yeshua could heal but the faith that healed her was faith that Yeshua was the Messiah!

E. The hem or corner of a garment has prophetic significance for Yeshua's return as well.

> Zec 8:23 This is what the LORD Almighty says: "In those days ten men from all languages and nations will take firm hold of one Jew by the hem of his robe and say, 'Let us go with you, because we have heard that God is with you.'" (NIV)

The Hebrew word for the phrase "hem of his robe" is again, Kan-aph meaning corner of a garment. The men from all nations were to take firm hold of the corner of his garment, the place where the tassel is connected. Those that "take hold" were showing three things.

1. Their faith in Yeshua as Messiah. Just like the woman with the issue of blood, they will proclaim that Yeshua has healing in His wings.

> Heb 3:14 We have come to share in Christ if we hold firmly till the end the confidence we had at first. (NIV)

2. Remembrance of the commands of God. The tassels were to "…remember all the commandments of the LORD and do them."

> Isa 14:1 For the LORD will have mercy on Jacob, and will still choose Israel, and settle them in their own land. The strangers will be joined with them, and they will cling to the house of Jacob. (NKJV)

Mic 4:1-2 Now it shall come to pass in the latter days That the mountain of the LORD'S house Shall be established on the top of the mountains, And shall be exalted above the hills; And peoples shall flow to it. 2 Many nations shall come and say, "Come, and let us go up to the mountain of the LORD, To the house of the God of Jacob; He will teach us His ways, And we shall walk in His paths." For out of Zion the law (Torah) shall go forth, And the word of the LORD from Jerusalem. (NKJV)

The Gentiles will be joined to Israel, go up with them to Jerusalem and God's Temple where Yeshua will teach us God's commandments as defined by His Torah!

Hebrew word picture: tzit-tzit: ציצת from right to left:

Tsadik: catch
Yood: closed hand, deed or action
Tsadik: catch
Tav: Mark or sign, specifically the mark of the covenant

"Catch, with your hand and by your deeds, catch the mark of the covenant".
"Take firm hold of the covenant by your deeds."

James reminds us that Abraham was counted righteous as his deeds followed his faith.

Jas 2:21 Was not our ancestor Abraham considered righteous for what he did when he offered his son Isaac on the altar? 22 You see that his faith and his actions were working together, and his faith was made complete by what he did. 26 As the body without the spirit is dead, so faith without deeds is dead. (NIV)

3. Their origin from all languages and nations. If we take this phrase literally, according to Genesis 10, there are seventy nations descended from Noah. Ten men from all seventy nations total seven hundred men for every Jew! There are currently about twelve million Jews in the world. Seven hundred times 12 million equals 8.4 billion. That's just about everybody.

Isa 45:22-23 "Look to Me, and be saved, All you ends of the earth! For I am God, and there is no other. 23 I have sworn by Myself; The word has gone out of My mouth in righteousness, And shall not return, That to Me every knee shall bow, Every tongue shall take an oath. (NKJV)

Let's grasp Yeshua's tzit-zit showing our faith in Him as Messiah. Let's proclaim that we heard God is with Him. Let's go with Him up to Jerusalem!

Php 2:9 Therefore God also has highly exalted Him and given Him the name which is above every name, 10 that at the name of Jesus every knee should bow, of those in heaven, and of those on earth, and of those under the earth, 11 and that every tongue should confess that Jesus Christ is Lord, to the glory of God the Father. (NKJV)

Student Notes for the Hem of the Garment

A. A woman touched the hem of Yeshua's garment and was healed. (Mat 9:20-22, Nu 15:38)

Hem: #2899. **kraspedon** kras'-ped-on of uncertain derivation; a margin, i.e. (specially), a fringe or tassel:--border, hem.

Tassel: #6734 ציצת tsiytsith, tsee-tseeth' feminine of #6731; a floral or wing-like projection, i.e. a forelock of hair, a tassel:--fringe, lock.

#6731 ציץ tsiyts, tseets or tsits {tseets}; from #6692; properly, glistening, i.e. a burnished plate; also a flower (as bright-colored); a wing (as gleaming in the air):--blossom, flower, plate, wing.

A better translation of the verse in Matthew would be:

B. What are the tzit-tzit? (Nu 15:39-41)

    1. Tallit

    2. Blue thread

Bue: #8504. תכלת techelet, tek-ay'-leth probably for #7827; the cerulean mussel, i.e. the color (violet) obtained therefrom or stuff dyed therewith:--blue.

This color of blue is used throughout the tabernacle. (Ex 26:1, 4, 31-33, Ex 27:16)

The high priest's garments contained the same blue (Ex 28:4-6, Ex 28:31, Ex 39:22)

3. Probable source of blue dye.

4. Connection with the Priesthood. (Ex 19:6)

C. The Heavenly pattern (Ex 25:9, Ex 25:40, Heb 8:1-5)

Remember and do all God's commandments (Nu 15:39-40, Joh 14:15, Joh 14:23, 1Jo 5:3, 1Pe 1:13-16)

D. Why is it important that the woman touched the tassel not just the hem or any other part of Yeshua's garment? (Mal 4:2, Mat 9:21-22)

A title of Messiah is _____

He has the characteristic of _____

Wings: #3671. כָּנָף kanaph, kaw- from #3670; an edge or extremity; specifically (of a bird or army) a wing, (of a garment or bed-clothing) a flap, (of the earth) a quarter, (of a building) a pinnacle:--+ bird, border, corner, end, feather(-ed), overspreading, X quarters, skirt, X sort, uttermost part, wing((-ed)).

E. Grasp the hem of a Jew (Zec 8:23)

"Hem of his robe" is Kan-aph.

Those that "take hold" were showing three things.
   1. Their faith in Messiah (Heb 3:14)

   2. Their remembrance of the commands of God: (Isa14:1, Mic 4:1-2, Ja 2:21-22, 26)

Hebrew word picture: tzit-tzit: ציצת from right to left:

Tsadik: צ fish-hook, catch

Yood: י closed hand, deed or action

Tsadik: צ fish-hook, catch

Tav: ת Mark or sign, specifically the mark of the covenant

"Catch, with your hand and by your deeds; catch the mark of the covenant".
"Take firm hold of the covenant by your deeds."

---

   3. Their origin from all languages and nations (Isa 45:22-23, Php 2:9-11)

Discussion Questions for the Hem of the Garment

1. Many people struggle with the reality that Yeshua was Jewish and followed all the commandments given in the Torah. Mark 14:55-56 tells us that the chief priests and the Sanhedrin could find no true witnesses against Yeshua. With that in mind, look up the following verses and discuss Yeshua's dress and daily practices as regarding each of the following.

    A. Wearing of tefillin (arm and forehead lacings): (Ex 13:9, Deu 6:8, Mat 23:5)

    B. Observation of the Feasts of the LORD: (Le 23:1-3, Lu 2:41-42, Joh 3:13, Joh 5:1, Joh 7:2-10, Joh 12:1)

    C. Observation of the Statutes: (Ex 13:2, Ex 13:14, Le 12:1-8, Lu 2:21-24)

    D. Observation of the Sabbath: (Ge 2:2-3, Ex 20:8-11, Lu 4:16, Lu 6:1-11)

2. Reread Numbers 15:37-41. What is the purpose for wearing the tzit-tzit (tassels)? Why is this important?

3. God gave the commandment to wear the tzit-tzit right after the congregation had to stone a man for violating the Sabbath (Nu 15:32-36). What does this tell you about the heart of God? (Read also 2Pe 3:9-12) What does this tell us about how seriously we should take holiness?

4. Other people were also healed after touching Yeshua's tzit-tzit (Mat 14:36). How can we symbolically reach out and touch Yeshua's tzit-tzit?

5. Zechariah 8:23 contains the idea of taking a firm hold of one Jew. The Hebrew word picture for tzit-tzit contains the idea of taking a firm hold of the covenant. How do these apply to taking a firm hold of Yeshua?

The Ashes of the Red Heifer

The Jewish sages divide observance of Torah into four different categories; the civil/legal commands, the moral/ethical commands, the "hedge" around the commands so that one doesn't accidentally violate Torah, and the decrees of God that have no logical reason. In examining the decrees of God that seem to have no logical reason, we invariably find that God is showing a pattern of redemption. This is the case for the ritual of purification required when someone became unclean through contact with the dead. How does sprinkling a person with water containing the ashes of a Red Heifer, cedar wood and scarlet wool possibly achieve ritual cleanness? It sounds more like superstitious magic! In reality, God uses it to paint a picture of His redemption plan. Take a few minutes and read Numbers chapter 19.

God is all about life. Nowhere in the creation account does God speak and bring about death. He speaks and brings forth life.

> Ge 2:9 And out of the ground the LORD God made every tree grow that is pleasant to the sight and good for food. The tree of life was also in the midst of the garden, and the tree of the knowledge of good and evil. (NKJV)

> Ge 2:16 And the LORD God commanded the man, saying, "Of every tree of the garden you may freely eat; 17 "but of the tree of the knowledge of good and evil you shall not eat, for in the day that you eat of it you shall surely die." (NKJV)

Adam was allowed to eat from the tree of life. There was no tree of death. Death came through eating of the tree of the knowledge of good and evil. By choosing to eat of the fruit of the forbidden tree, Adam and Eve chose to disobey God—they chose to decide for themselves what is good and evil. That sin brought about the corruption and deterioration of the body with the ultimate corruption found in death.

> Ge 3:6 So when the woman saw that the tree was good for food, that it was pleasant to the eyes, and a tree desirable to make one wise, she took of its fruit and ate. She also gave to her husband with her, and he ate. (NKJV)

SHE decided the tree was good for food; SHE decided it was pleasant to the eyes; SHE decided the fruit would make one wise; SHE decided to eat. Her husband, who was with her, also DECIDED and ate the fruit.

> Ge 3:22 Then the LORD God said, "Behold, the man has become like one of Us, to know good and evil. And now, lest he put out his hand and take also of the tree of life, and eat, and live forever" - 23 therefore the LORD God sent him out of the garden of Eden to till the ground from which he was taken. (NKJV)

Through the purification ritual of the ashes of the Red Heifer, God shows how we can pass from death into eternal life. The Slaughter of the Red heifer and its use in purification for touching a dead body is symbolic of Yeshua's crucifixion and how his blood cleanses us from sin, thus allowing us to pass from death into life.

> Joh 5:24 "Most assuredly, I say to you, he who hears My word and believes in Him who sent Me has everlasting life, and shall not come into judgment, but has passed from death into life. (NKJV)

A. Both were without blemish.
   1. The Red Heifer was without blemish.

> Nu 19:2 "This is the ordinance of the law which the LORD has commanded, saying: 'Speak to the children of Israel, that they bring you a red heifer without blemish, in which there is no defect and on which a yoke has never come. NKJV)

   2. Yeshua was without blemish.

> 1Pe 1:18 knowing that you were not redeemed with corruptible things, like silver or gold, from your aimless conduct received by tradition from your fathers, 19 but with the precious blood of Christ, as of a lamb without blemish and without spot. (NKJV)

B. Both were not to be yoked.
   1. The Red Heifer had never been used as a "servant" of man by pulling a plow or cart. See Numbers 19:2 above. The heifer was never to have worn a yoke.

   2. The only "master" Yeshua had was the Father. He was "not under yoke" to man's authority but only God's authority. Unlike Adam and Eve, He chose to obey God His Father.

> Joh 5:30 "I can of Myself do nothing. As I hear, I judge; and My judgment is righteous, because I do not seek My own will but the will of the Father who sent Me. (NKJV)

> Joh 6:38 "For I have come down from heaven, not to do My own will, but the will of Him who sent Me. (NKJV)

Although Yeshua was tempted, He was without sin and thus, not subject to the law of sin and death.

> Heb 4:15 For we do not have a High Priest who cannot sympathize with our weaknesses, but was in all points tempted as we are, yet without sin. (NKJV)

We, however, are subject to the law of sin and death. It is only through the purification we have in Yeshua that we are free from the corruption of death.

Ro 7:21 I find then a law, that evil is present with me, the one who wills to do good. 22 For I delight in the law of God according to the inward man. 23 But I see another law in my members, warring against the law of my mind, and bringing me into captivity to the law of sin which is in my members. (NKJV)

Ro 8:2 For the law of the Spirit of life in Christ Jesus has made me free from the law of sin and death. (NKJV)

C. Both were killed outside the camp. Notice that it wasn't just outside the tent of meeting which contained the tabernacle, but outside the camp!
1. The Red heifer:

Nu 19:3 And ye shall give her unto Eleazar the priest, that he may bring her forth without the camp, and one shall slay her before his face: (KJV)

2. Yeshua was killed outside the camp. Since all of Jerusalem is holy to the LORD, that would be outside the city.

Heb 13:12 Therefore Jesus also, that He might sanctify the people with His own blood, suffered outside the gate. (NKJV)

Nehemiah refers to Jerusalem as the holy city at the time of the return from the Babylonian exile.

Neh 11:1 Now the leaders of the people dwelt at Jerusalem; the rest of the people cast lots to bring one out of ten to dwell in Jerusalem, the holy city, and nine-tenths were to dwell in other cities. (NKJV)

D. Both were slain before the face of God.
1. Eleazar was to slay the heifer "before his face." Whose face? In Numbers 19:3 above, the word for the phrase "before his face" is # 6440 paniym, paw-neem', the face; from #6437 panah, paw-naw', a primitive root; to turn; by implication to face. In Leviticus the instructions for all the offerings included the provision that they were to be done before the LORD. The sacrifices were to be killed facing the tabernacle. When the temple was built, they were to be facing the holy of holies. The temple faced east with the altar outside the Holy place directly in front of the door. The temple doors were open at the time of the sacrifices and the veil that enclosed the Holy of Holies was visible from the altar.

Le 1:3 If his offering be a burnt sacrifice of the herd, let him offer a male without blemish: he shall offer it of his own voluntary will at the door of the tabernacle of the congregation before (paniym) the LORD. (KJV)

Le 3:7 If he offer a lamb for his offering, then shall he offer it before (paniym) the LORD. (KJV)

Le 6:25 Speak unto Aaron and to his sons, saying, This is the law of the sin offering: In the place where the burnt offering is killed shall the sin offering be killed before (paniym) the LORD: it is most holy. (KJV)

In order for the Red Heifer to be killed outside the camp but before the LORD, the slaughter would have had to be on the Mt. of Olives. According to the Mishna a bridge was built - "arches upon arches" - to take the cow over the cemetery in the Kidron Valley, to the Mount of Anointing (Mount of Olives) where it would be burned. The ashes of the red heifer were necessary to make people ritually pure so they could enter the sacred area of the Temple Mount. (Jerusalem Post May 31, 2001)

The Red heifer was slaughtered on the Mt. of Olives facing the temple. Because the Mt. of Olives is in a direct line of sight about 200 feet higher in elevation, the veil enclosing the Holy of Holies could be seen from the mount.

2. Yeshua had to have been crucified before the face of God to fulfill the pattern of the sacrifices and the killing of the Red Heifer.

It is very likely that Yeshua was crucified on the Mt. of Olives looking across the Kidron valley, the valley of the shadow of death, looking directly toward the Temple before His Father's Face. When Yeshua cries out to God, He could have been looking at the Holy of Holies.

Mat 27:46 And about the ninth hour Jesus cried with a loud voice, saying, Eli, Eli, lama sabachthani? that is to say, My God, my God, why hast thou forsaken me? (KJV)

Interestingly enough, the guards watching Yeshua **saw** those things that were done.

Mat 27:50 Jesus, when he had cried again with a loud voice, yielded up the ghost. 51 And, behold, the veil of the temple was rent in twain from the top to the bottom; and the earth did quake, and the rocks rent; 52 And the graves were opened; and many bodies of the saints which slept arose, 53 And came out of the graves after his resurrection, and went into the holy city, and appeared unto many. 54 Now when the centurion, and they that were with him, watching Jesus, **saw the earthquake, and those things that were done**, they feared greatly, saying, Truly this was the Son of God. (KJV)

What did they see besides the earthquake? The bodies of the saints did not come out of their graves until after the resurrection. Could they have seen the veil torn in two? Much of the Mt. of Olives is covered with graves, could they have seen the graves "opened," that is, disturbed by the earthquake? Could Golgotha be a specific place on the Mt. of Olives?

Golgotha is the Aramaic word for skull. The Hebrew equivalent is gulgoleth.

160

Head: #1538. גלגלת gulgoleth, gul-go'-leth a skull (as round); by implication, a head (in enumeration of persons):--head, every man, poll, skull.

Each Jewish man had to pay a temple tax of one bekah a head (gulgoleth) each year as established by Exodus 38:25-26.

> Ex 38:25 And the silver from those who were numbered of the congregation was one hundred talents and one thousand seven hundred and seventy-five shekels, according to the shekel of the sanctuary: 26 a bekah for each man (gulgoleth) (that is, half a shekel, according to the shekel of the sanctuary), for everyone included in the numbering from twenty years old and above, for six hundred and three thousand, five hundred and fifty men. (NKJV)

At the time of Yeshua, the place where the people registered for the "temple tax" was on the northern slopes of the Mt. of Olives near the place where the sin offering was taken outside the camp to be burned. Ezekiel refers to it as the appointed place. In Hebrew, this is the word "miphkad."

> Eze 43:21 Thou shalt take the bullock also of the sin offering, and he shall burn it in the appointed place (miphkad) of the house, without the sanctuary. (KJV)

Nehemiah refers to the gate that led to the appointed place as the Miphkad Gate located on the Northeast side of the city.

> Neh 3:31 After him repaired Malchiah the goldsmith's son unto the place of the Nethinims, and of the merchants, over against the gate Miphkad, and to the going up of the corner. (KJV)

Here, at the place of the gulgoleth outside the city gate on the Mt. of Olives, people registered for the temple tax. The priests used this same Miphkad Gate to take the red heifer to the Mt. of Olives and to take away the scapegoat on Yom Kippur (See Leviticus 16). Golgotha is a specific place on the Mt. of Olives.

E. The priest sprinkles the blood in the same way that the blood is sprinkled on Yom Kippur, the Day of Atonement.

> Nu 19:4 'and Eleazar the priest shall take some of its blood with his finger, and sprinkle some of its blood seven times directly in front of the tabernacle of meeting. (NKJV)

> Le 16:14 "He shall take some of the blood of the bull and sprinkle it with his finger on the mercy seat on the east side; and before the mercy seat he shall sprinkle some of the blood with his finger seven times. (NKJV)

F. The elements represent the crucifixion.

> Nu 19:6 'And the priest shall take cedar wood and hyssop and scarlet, and cast them into the midst of the fire burning the heifer. (NKJV)

The cedar is a wood that is resistant to decay. The cedars of Lebanon were used to build Solomon's temple. If one wants to preserve garments, they are put into a cedar chest. There is a reason a bride's "Hope chest" was always made of cedar! The fragrance of cedar is opposite to that of decay. It represents the body of Messiah that did not decay in the grave as well as the cross upon which He is crucified. The scarlet wool is the blood of the lamb. The hyssop was used to apply the blood on the doorposts at Passover.

> Ex 12:22 And ye shall take a bunch of hyssop, and dip it in the blood that is in the basin, and strike the lintel and the two side posts with the blood that is in the basin; and none of you shall go out at the door of his house until the morning. (KJV)

The same elements were used to seal the covenant between God and the Israelites at Sinai. And these are merely a copy of the real temple in heaven.

> Heb 9:19 For when Moses had spoken every precept to all the people according to the law, he took the blood of calves and goats, with water, scarlet wool, and hyssop, and sprinkled both the book itself and all the people, 20 saying, "This is the blood of the covenant which God has commanded you." 21 Then likewise he sprinkled with blood both the tabernacle and all the vessels of the ministry. 22 And according to the law almost all things are purified with blood, and without shedding of blood there is no remission. 23 Therefore it was necessary that the copies of the things in the heavens should be purified with these, but the heavenly things themselves with better sacrifices than these. 24 For Christ has not entered the holy places made with hands, which are copies of the true, but into heaven itself, now to appear in the presence of God for us; (NKJV)

G. All the priests who participated in preparing the ashes of the Red heifer had to be clean to start with and in the process became unclean. There are many ways to become unclean; sin is only one of them. A person who is unclean cannot go into the tabernacle or temple. For many kinds of uncleanness, all that is needed is to wash oneself and/or one's clothes, wait until evening, and then one is clean again. See Leviticus chapter 15 for various examples.

> Nu 19:7 'Then the priest shall wash his clothes, he shall bathe in water, and afterward he shall come into the camp; the priest shall be unclean until evening. 8 'And the one who burns it shall wash his clothes in water, bathe in water, and shall be unclean until evening. 9 'Then a man who is clean shall gather up the ashes of the heifer, and store them outside the camp in a clean place; and they shall be kept for the congregation of the children of Israel for the water of purification; it is for purifying from sin. 10 'And the one who gathers the ashes of the heifer shall wash his clothes, and be unclean until evening. It shall be a statute forever to the children of Israel and to the stranger who dwells among them. (NKJV)

When Yeshua took on our sins, He became unclean for us.

> 2Co 5:21 For He made Him who knew no sin to be sin for us, that we might become the righteousness of God in Him. (NKJV)

This is why we hear Yeshua cry out on the cross. When Yeshua became sin, he was no longer clean and could not be in the presence of God.

> Mat 27:46 And about the ninth hour Jesus cried out with a loud voice, saying, "Eli, Eli, lama sabachthani?" that is, "My God, My God, why have You forsaken Me?" (NKJV)

This is also another reason why His crucifixion had to be outside the city. Nothing unclean is to enter the holy city of Jerusalem.

> Isa 52:1 Awake, awake! Put on your strength, O Zion; Put on your beautiful garments, O Jerusalem, the holy city! For the uncircumcised and the unclean Shall no longer come to you. (NKJV)

H. The first purification takes place on the third day.

> Nu 19:12 'He shall purify himself with the water on the **third day** and on the seventh day; then he will be clean. But if he does not purify himself on the third day and on the seventh day, he will not be clean. 13 'Whoever touches the body of anyone who has died, and does not purify himself, defiles the tabernacle of the LORD. That person shall be cut off from Israel. He shall be unclean, because the water of purification was not sprinkled on him; his uncleanness is still on him. (NKJV)

On the third day, Yeshua rose again.

> Ac 10:39 "And we are witnesses of all things which He did both in the land of the Jews and in Jerusalem, whom they killed by hanging on a tree. 40 "Him God raised up on the third day, and showed Him openly, (NKJV)

> Lu 24:21 "But we were hoping that it was He who was going to redeem Israel. Indeed, besides all this, today is the third day since these things happened. 22 "Yes, and certain women of our company, who arrived at the tomb early, astonished us. 23 "When they did not find His body, they came saying that they had also seen a vision of angels who said He was alive. (NKJV)

I. The ashes of the Red heifer are used to cleanse a person from contact with a dead body.

> Nu 19:17 'And for an unclean person they shall take some of the ashes of the heifer burnt for purification from sin, and running water shall be put on them in a vessel. 18 'A clean person shall take hyssop and dip it in the water, sprinkle it on the tent,

on all the vessels, on the persons who were there, or on the one who touched a bone, the slain, the dead, or a grave. 19 'The clean person shall sprinkle the unclean on the third day and on the seventh day; and on the seventh day he shall purify himself, wash his clothes, and bathe in water; and at evening he shall be clean. (NKJV)

Contact with a dead body symbolically connects a person with the original sin which caused corruption and decay to enter the world. Thus, one is unable to approach God who is the very essence of life. Sin in our lives brings death; those living in sin are dead already.

Ro 5:12 Therefore, just as through one man sin entered the world, and death through sin, and thus death spread to all men, because all sinned-- 13 (For until the law sin was in the world, but sin is not imputed when there is no law. 14 Nevertheless death reigned from Adam to Moses, even over those who had not sinned according to the likeness of the transgression of Adam, who is a type of Him who was to come. (NKJV)

Ro 8:10 And if Christ is in you, the body is dead because of sin, but the Spirit is life because of righteousness. (NKJV)

The ritual of the ashes of the Red Heifer points to the purifying work of the blood of Christ.

Heb 9:13 For if the blood of bulls and goats and the **ashes of a heifer**, sprinkling the unclean, sanctifies for the purifying of the flesh, (NKJV) 14 how much more shall the blood of Christ, who through the eternal Spirit offered Himself without spot to God, cleanse your conscience from dead works to serve the living God? (NKJV)

J. The seventh day speaks of completion. On the seventh day God rested. The end of the feast season is in the seventh month. The length of the Feast of unleavened Bread and the Feast of Tabernacles is seven days. Yeshua died on Passover, the eve of the Feast of Unleavened Bread. He rose from the dead on the third day of the Feast, becoming the firstfruits from the dead. The seventh day completed the Feast of Unleavened Bread. The very name of the Feast suggests incorruptibility—unleavened bread does not decay! The seventh day is about the first resurrection—the resurrection of the saints.

This meaning was not lost on Paul. In 1 Corinthians, Paul explains the doctrine of the resurrection from the dead. In this chapter, he refers to this ritual when he writes about baptism for the dead.

1Co 15:29 Otherwise, what will they do who are baptized for the dead, if the dead do not rise at all? Why then are they baptized for the dead? (NKJV)

A baptism is a ceremonial cleansing. The word "baptize" means to submerge, to wash.

Baptize: #907. βαπτιζω baptizo, bap-tid'-zo from a derivative of 911; to immerse, submerge; to make whelmed (i.e. fully wet)

There are two ceremonial cleansings associated with the dead. One is the washing of the body, a sort of last cleansing to prepare the body for resurrection. The second is the ceremonial washing after the ritual of purification with the ashes of the Red Heifer. In Numbers 19:19 above, the unclean person finished the ritual on the seventh day by bathing in water.

Paul says if there is no resurrection from the dead, then there is no reason for the dead body to be washed. If there is no reason to wash the dead body, there is no reason for a person to become ritually unclean for doing so. Therefore, the sprinkling of the ashes of the Red Heifer and washing with water on the seventh day would be meaningless.

Because of Yeshua's resurrection on the third day, we are alive in Christ. This is the promise of the sprinkling on the third day.

> Ro 6:11 Likewise you also, reckon yourselves to be dead indeed to sin, but alive to God in Christ Jesus our Lord. (NKJV)

Because of the sprinkling of the ashes on the seventh day, we can be confident in our own resurrection.

> 1Co 15:22 For as in Adam all die, even so in Christ all shall be made alive. (NKJV)

Corruption, in the form of death, comes because of Adam; incorruption in the form of eternal life comes through Yeshua our Messiah.

> 1Co 15:51 Behold, I tell you a mystery: We shall not all sleep, but we shall all be changed--52 in a moment, in the twinkling of an eye, at the last trumpet. For the trumpet will sound, and the dead will be raised incorruptible, and we shall be changed. 53 For this corruptible must put on incorruption, and this mortal must put on immortality. 54 So when this corruptible has put on incorruption, and this mortal has put on immortality, then shall be brought to pass the saying that is written: "Death is swallowed up in victory." 55 "O Death, where is your sting? O Hades, where is your victory?" (NKJV)

Student Notes for the Ashes of the Red Heifer

The Jewish sages divide observance of Torah into four different categories; the civil/legal commands, the moral/ethical commands, the "hedge" around the commands so that one doesn't accidentally violate Torah, and the decrees of God that have no logical reason. In examining the decrees of God that seem to have no logical reason, we invariably find that God is showing a pattern of redemption.

Read Numbers chapter 19.

A. God is all about life. (Ge 2:9,16)

1. Death came through eating of the tree of the knowledge of good and evil. (Ge 3:6, 22-23)

2. Through the purification ritual of the ashes of the Red Heifer, God shows how we can pass from death into eternal life. (Joh 5:24)

B. Both were without blemish.
   1. The Red Heifer was without blemish. (Nu 19:2)

   2. Yeshua was without blemish. (1Pe 1:18-19)

C. Both were not to be yoked.
   1. The Red Heifer: (refer to Nu 19:2 above)

   2. The only "master" Yeshua had was the Father. (Joh 5:30, Joh 6:38)

3. The Law of sin and death (Heb 4:15, Ro 7:21-23, Ro 8:2)

D. Both were killed outside the camp.
　　1. The Red heifer: (Nu 19:3)

　　2. Yeshua was killed outside the camp. (Heb 13:12, Neh 11:1)

E. Both were slain before the face of God.
　　1. Eleazar was to slay the heifer "before his face." Whose face? (Refer to Nu. 19:3 above, Le 1:3, Le 3:7, Le 6:25)

"Before his face": Strong's # 6440 paniym, paw-neem', The face; from #6437 panah, paw-naw', a primitive root; to turn; by implication to face.

　　2. Outside the camp but before the LORD: Mishna:

　　3. Possible site for Yeshua's crucifixion: Outside the camp but before the LORD (Mat 27:46, 50-54)

4. The place of the skull: (Ex 38:25-26, Eze 43:21, Neh 3:31)
Head: #1538. גלגלת gulgoleth, gul-go'-leth a skull (as round); by implication, a head (in enumeration of persons):--head, every man, poll, skull.

F. The priest sprinkles the blood in the same way that the blood is sprinkled on Yom Kippur, the Day of Atonement. (Nu 19:4, Le 16:14)

G. The elements represent the crucifixion. (Nu 19:6, Ex 12:22, Heb 9:19-24)

Cedar:

The scarlet wool:

The hyssop:

H. All the priests went from clean to unclean: (Nu 19:7-10, 2Co 5:21, Mat 27:46, Isa 52:1)

I. The third day. (Nu 19:12-13, Ac 10:39-40, Lu 24:21-23)

J. The ritual of the ashes of the Red Heifer points to the purifying work of the blood of Messiah. (Nu 19:17-19, Ro 5:12-14, Ro 8:10, Heb 9:13-14)

K. The seventh day speaks of completion.

    1. Seventh day symbolism:

    2. Baptism for the dead. (1 Cor. 15:29, refer to Nu 19:19 above)

Baptize: #907. βαπτιζω baptizo, bap-tid'-zo from a derivative of 911; to immerse, submerge; to make whelmed (i.e. fully wet)

If there is no resurrection from the dead, then _____

If there is no reason to wash the dead body, then _____

Finally, _____

    3. The promise of the sprinkling on the third day. (Ro 6:11)

    4. The promise of the sprinkling of the ashes on the seventh day (1Co 15:22, 1Co 15:51-55)

Discussion Questions for the Red Heifer

1. The purification with the ashes of the Red Heifer is all about purifying from the corruption of death. In 1 Corinthians 15:26, Paul writes that death is the last enemy. How is death an enemy? Support your answer with scriptures.

2. Hebrews 9:11-14 says that both the rituals of Yom Kippur and sprinkling for the dead serve to purify the flesh and compare them to the atoning blood of Messiah. Compare the purposes of these two rituals.

3. Read Leviticus 15 which details many ways a person can become unclean. How do they all refer to the mortality of man; that is his corruptible body?

4. How is the ritual of purification by the sprinkling of the ashes of the Red Heifer a reminder of the fallen state of mankind and the need for a redeemer?

5. The entire chapter of 1 Corinthians 15 is a reassurance that there will be a resurrection of the dead. How does understanding the ritual of purification by the sprinkling of the ashes of the Red Heifer help to understand this chapter?

6. What are some of the events in Yeshua's life, resurrection or second coming that are associated with the Mt. of Olives? Discuss whether you think these events add evidence to the possibility that Yeshua's crucifixion may have taken place on the Mt. of Olives.

172

Appendix A: The Hebrew Alphabet

The Hebrew alphabet started out in the form of pictographs with each character representing a specific picture. Words were constructed by putting pictures together illustrating a characteristic of a word. An example is the word "father." The Hebrew word for father is spelled "ab" in English. In Hebrew it consists of the letters aleph, א, and bet, ב written from right to left, אב. From the Hebrew alphabet chart we see that the aleph represents an ox for strength or leadership and the bet represents a family or house. A father, therefore, is the strength and leader of his house and family.

The Hebrew letters also stand for numbers. There weren't different symbols for numbers. Many numbers have significance in scripture. We see numbers repeated over and over. For example, one is the number for God, seven is the number of completion, eight is the number of new beginnings, and forty is the number of testing or trial.

Even as the shape of the letters changed and became more abstract, the connection to the original picture language remains. Moses would have written in the pictograph or early ancient Hebrew form; David in the mid ancient Hebrew; and Yeshua would have written in the late ancient Hebrew form. The Modern Hebrew script was not established until the 15th century A.D. and was strongly influenced by the Aramaic form of the letters.

When we read the Old Testament of the Bible, we need to realize that it was originally written in ancient Hebrew and each of the letters in the words represents a picture. Many words and names carry extra, deeper meaning by examining the word picture presented by the original pictographs. Yeshua said that "not one jot or tittle" would pass away from the word of God.

> Mat 5:18 "For assuredly, I say to you, till heaven and earth pass away, one jot or one tittle will by no means pass from the law till all is fulfilled. (NKJV)

The jot refers to the smallest Hebrew letter the yad or yood, י. A tittle is a variation in how a letter is written. Some examples of a "tittle" would be a letter that is written larger or smaller than normal, a gap in the text, a word spelled with an additional letter or a letter left out, as well as embellishments of a letter. All those variations in text are for a purpose with the ultimate purpose to further reveal the character of God.

> 2Ti 2:15 Study to shew thyself approved unto God, a workman that needeth not to be ashamed, rightly dividing the word of truth. (KJV)

> Pr 25:2 It is the glory of God to conceal a matter, But the glory of kings is to search out a matter. (NKJV)

> 2Ti 3:16 All Scripture is given by inspiration of God, and is profitable for doctrine, for reproof, for correction, for instruction in righteousness, (NKJV)

Hebrew Alphabet Chart

Ancient Hebrew Early	Mid	Late	Sound	Name	Literal and symbolic meaning	Modern Script	End of Word	Numeric value	End of word character
𓃾	⊀	א	silent	aleph	ox, bull – strength, leader, first	א		1	
⊔	⊿	⊐	b, bh, v	beyt (bet)	tent, house – household, into, family	ב		2	
⌐	⌐	⌐	g	gimel	camel – pride, to lift up, animal	ג		3	
⊳	⊲	⊲	d	dalet	door – pathway, enter	ד		4	
𐤄	⊒	⊓	h, e	hey	window, lattice – "the", to reveal	ה		5	
Υ	Υ	⊦	w, o, u	vav	nail – "and", to secure, to add	ו		6	
⊨	⊨	⊏	z	zayin	weapon – cut, to cut off	ז		7	
⊞	⊞	⊓	h	het	fence, a chamber – private, to separate	ח		8	
⊗	⊗	⊘	th	tet	to twist, a snake – to surround	ט		9	
⊿	⊿	⊿	y, i	yad (yood)	hand, closed hand – a deed, to make, work	י		10	
⊎	⊎	⊐	k, kh	kaph	arm, open hand – to cover, to allow, to open	כ	ך	20	500
∪	∪	∪	l	lamed	cattle goad, staff – prod, toward, control, authority	ל		30	
⊠	⊠	⊼	m	Mem	water – massive, chaos, liquid	מ	ם	40	600
⊂	⊂	⊂	n	nun (noon)	fish (moving) – activity, life	נ	ן	50	700
≢	≢	⊃	s	samech	a prop – support, turn	ס		60	
⊘	⊘	⊘	silent	ayin	eye – to see, know, experience	ע		70	
⊘	⌐	⌐	p, ph	pey	mouth – to speak, to open, a word	פ	ף	80	800
⊰	⊰	⊢	ts	tsadik	fish hook – harvest, need, desire	צ	ץ	90	900
⏀	⏀	⊅	q	quph (koof)	back of the head – behind, the last, the least	ק		100	
⊲	⊲	⊓	r	resh	head – a person, highest, the head	ר		200	
⊟	⊟	⊵	sh	shin	teeth – consume, destroy	ש		300	
⊤	×	⊓	t	tav	a sign, a cross – to covenant, to seal	ת		400	

Appendix B: Tying the Tzitzit According to Rabbinic Tradition

It is a positive commandment to put tzitzit on any four cornered garment that you wear, as it says in Numbers:

> Nu 15:37 Again the LORD spoke to Moses, saying, 38 "Speak to the children of Israel: Tell them to make tassels on the corners of their garments throughout their generations, and to put a blue thread in the tassels of the corners. 39 "And you shall have the tassel, that you may look upon it and remember all the commandments of the LORD and do them, and that you may not follow the harlotry to which your own heart and your own eyes are inclined, 40 "and that you may remember and do all My commandments, and be holy for your God. 41 "I am the LORD your God, who brought you out of the land of Egypt, to be your God: I am the LORD your God." (NKJV)

According to rabbinic tradition this commandment is given in order to remember God, His great love, all of His commandments and to do them. While the large tallit is the garment usually associated with the Tzitzit and used specifically for prayer, the commandment in Numbers is to wear a garment with tzitzit all day every day. Traditional Jews, therefore, wear a tallit katan or small tallit as an under garment all day and a large tallit just for morning prayers. The tzitzit are to be attached at the corners. A general guide is that there be a hole three or four finger breadths from the corner edges. The Tzitzit are tied in such a manner that they can be attached to the garment and removed when the garment is cleaned.

Before you try tying tzitzit to your tallit, it is advisable to practice with twine or other heavy string looped around a chair leg or other such stable object. The figure to the left shows a completed tzitzit.

In order to make Tzitzit removable from your tallit katan or other garment, you will need to devise a method to create a 3 to 4 inch loop at the top of your Tzitzit. This can be done several ways but the most common is to use a flat wooden board 18 to 24 inches long and place 2 nails partially inserted into the board 3 to 4 inches apart, one above the other, not side by side at one end of the board (Figure 1) Tradition says that the Tzitzit consists of either all white cords or at least one blue cord with the remainder being white. The scripture, however, only specifies that it contain one blue thread. One may find many different combinations of colors in a Tzitzit but by far the most common is the all white or blue and white.

Although you can spin or devise your own tzitzit strands (some will use heavy embroidery thread), it is easier to buy a tzitzit pack, which is available at most Hebrew bookstores or online. In the pack, there will be sixteen strands, four long ones and twelve short ones; four of aprox. 60 inches and twelve at aprox. 40 inches. Separate these into four groups with one long and three short in each. The longer strand is called the shammash and is the one used for the winding and is normally the blue one. Even up the

Figure 1

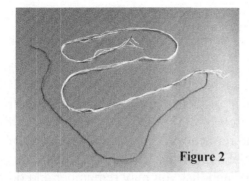

Figure 2

four strands at one end. This will leave one long strand, the shammash, extending below the other three (figure 2).

If you are intending to permanently attach your tzitzit to your large tallit, push the group through one of the corner holes in the tallit. Even them up on either side of the hole and you will now have eight strands (the original four now being doubled) and leave the extra length of the shammash hanging to one side. If you are making your tzitzit with the loop at the top, drape them around the top most of the two nails in the board, even up the three white strands so there is an even amount on each side of the nail (figure 3). To make them easier to handle and prevent them from slipping relative to each other, secure them by taping them to the board between the two nails with a removable tape such as painters masking tape; the blue stuff from 3M works very well (figure 4). This will leave you with four strands on each side of the nails, three white and one blue with one of the blue ones being the longer shammash strand.

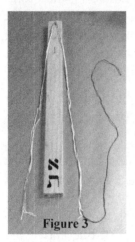

Figure 3

Figure 4

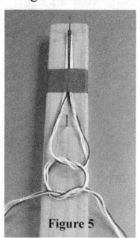

Figure 5

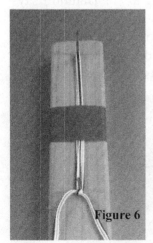

Figure 6

With four strands in one hand and the other four in the other hand, make a square knot near the edge of the tallit or just below the lower nail in the board cinching it up tight against the lower nail (figures 5 and 6). After you tie this first knot, take the shammash and wind it round the other seven strands in a spiral (seven turns). Be sure you end the winding where you began; otherwise you may end up with 8 or 6 winds. Make another square knot at this point (four strands over four strands, exactly the same as the first knot). (Figure 7) Spiral the shammash eight times around.

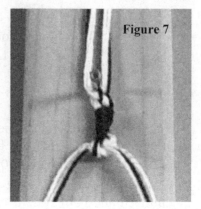

Figure 7

Square knot. Spiral the shammash eleven times around. Square knot. Spiral the shammash thirteen times around.

Final square knot. Leave the remaining cords, do not cut them (figure 8). Embroidery thread and some other types of cord tend to unravel at the ends. The ends of the cords can

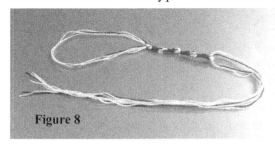

Figure 8

be sealed by dipping the ends in clear wax. If the shammash cord ends up considerably longer than the others, go ahead and trim it.

This is the common, traditional type of tying the Tzitzit. The symbolism for the numbers of spirals is central to the overall symbolism of the tzitzit. Seven and eight equals fifteen, which in gematria (numerology) is equal to the two letters yod and heh, the first two letters of the Name of God. Eleven is the equivalent of vav and heh, the last two letters of the Name of God. The total, twenty six, is thus equivalent and representative of the YHVH, the four-letter Name of God. Thirteen is equivalent to the Hebrew word Echad, spelled alef, chet, dalet which means One. So to look at the tzitzit is to remember and know that "God is One." There are, however, two variations on this:

1. A Sephardic tying method adds another dimension to the pattern: each time the shammash is brought around, take it under the previous wind before winding it further. This will produce a curving spiral-like ridge around the tzitzit (figure 9). This, too, should be practiced before trying it to a tallit.

2. Some tie the tzitzit with the shammash spiraling 10-5-6-5 times respectively instead of the 7-8-11-13 pattern. According to this way of winding, each section is a different letter of God's four letter Name. The Yod =10, Hey =5, Vav=6 and the Hey =5 (figure 10).

The central commandment surrounding the tzitzit is: "And you should see it and remember all of God's commandments and do them." How do the tzitzit do this? In gematria, the numbers of the letters of the word tzitzit equal six hundred. In addition there are eight strands plus five knots. The total is six hundred thirteen which according to tradition, is the exact number of commandments (mitzvot) in the Torah. Just to look at the tzitzit, therefore, is to remember all the mitzvot.

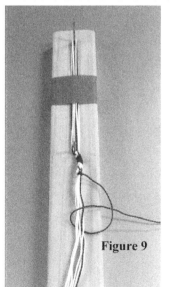

Figure 9

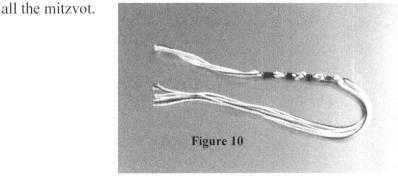

Figure 10

Appendix C: The Biblical Calendar

Events in prophecy are frequently tied to specific times of the year. We need to understand and be on the Biblical Calendar to truly understand and recognize the fulfillment of these prophecies. God tells us that one of the ways Satan will try to deceive the Saints is by changing the "appointed times."

> Da 7:25 And he shall speak great words against the most High, and shall wear out the saints of the most High, and **think to change times** and laws: and they shall be given into his hand until a time and times and the dividing of time. (KJV)

He has successfully done this by getting the whole world on the Gregorian calendar which observes only a solar year. God created both the sun and the moon as signs of the appointed times.

> Ge 1:14 And God said, Let there be lights in the firmament of the heaven to divide the day from the night; and let them be for signs, and for seasons, and for days, and years: (KJV)

The word translated as seasons is mo'ed meaning a fixed or set time, an appointed time. From the very beginning, God set up both the sun and the moon to mark His calendar.

1. The **Biblical Calendar** is based on the combined solar and lunar cycles. The months are determined by the lunar cycles and the length of the year by the solar cycles. The cycle of the moon is 29 and ½ days long. So, the months in the Jewish calendar alternate between 29 and 30 days long. Twelve months adds up to only 354 days. This is where the solar cycle comes in. The solar cycle is 365 and ¼ days long, just over 11 days longer than a strictly lunar year. To compensate for the extra length needed to make a complete year, the Biblical Calendar, like the Gregorian calendar, has leap years. Instead of having leap years that add a day, the Biblical calendar inserts whole months as "leap months." These occur on a 19- year cycle. A leap month is inserted every 3rd 6th, 8th, 11th, 14th 17th and 19th year before Adar, the last month of the religious calendar.

1	2	3	4	5	6	7	8	9	10	11	12	13	14	15	16	17	18	19
R	R	L	R	R	L	R	L	R	R	L	R	R	L	R	R	L	R	L

Today we simply look at a printed (or digital) calendar to determine what month it is. How did Israel determine months before printing or computers? Until the 4th century A.D. each new month had to be declared by the Sanhedrin (or the court of Israel). Witnesses would be stationed around Judea to watch for the new moon. The "new moon" in Biblical terms is not the total shadow, but the first sliver of the waxing moon. When the moon was sighted, the witnesses ran back to the Sanhedrin. Upon the arrival of the two witnesses and their testimony, the Sanhedrin would officially declare the beginning of the new month. To determine when to add a "leap" month, the priests checked the ripeness of the barley crop. If the barley was not almost ready to harvest, they declared a second month of Adar so the barley harvest always fell in Nisan.

There are actually two Biblical Calendars, a civil calendar and a religious calendar.

Civil calendar: This is the calendar used by modern day Jews. The first month, Tishrei begins in the fall. Jewish tradition believes that Tirhrei 1 is the day that God created Adam. The change in year number occurs at this time. Tishrei is referred to in scripture as the end of the year.

> De 31:10 And Moses commanded them, saying: "At the **end of every seven years**, at the appointed time in the year of release, at the Feast of Tabernacles...(NKJV)

Religious calendar: The First month is Nisan which is in the early spring. This is because Moses led the Israelites out of Egypt in the month of Nisan. It symbolizes new beginnings or new birth.

You can think of these two ways of counting within the Biblical Calendar as the difference between our own traditional calendar year and the school year. A school year begins in August or September and ends in May or June whereas the traditional year begins with January and ends with December. The months are all the same but the beginning and ending changes. See the chart below for how the Biblical Calendar numbers the months.

Biblical Calendar

Hebrew Name	Civil sequence#	Redemption sequence#	Gregorian equivalent
Tishrei	1	7	Sept-Oct
Chesvan	2	8	Oct-Nov
Kislev	3	9	Nov-Dec
Tevet	4	10	Dec-Jan
Shevat	5	11	Jan-Feb
Adar (I and II)	6	12	Feb-Mar
Nisan	7	1	Mar-Apr
Iyyar	8	2	Apr-May
Sivan	9	3	May-Jun
Tammuz	10	4	Jun-Jul
Av	11	5	Jul-Aug
Elul	12	6	Aug-Sep

Lastly, a few additional items about the Biblical Calendar are worth mentioning:

- Yom Kippur does not fall next to a Saturday.
- Hoshana Rabba (the seventh day of the Feast of Tabernacles) does not fall on a Saturday.
- Tishrei 1 is always on a Monday, Tuesday, Thursday or Saturday.

- The period between Nisan 1 and Tishrei 1 is always the same length.
- The period from Nisan 15 to Tishrei 22 (which encompasses all the Feasts of the LORD) is always 185 days. Incidentally, this is also the length of time between the spring and fall equinoxes.
- Years are counted from the beginning of creation so as of this writing it is 5769 (versus 2009)
- Days are counted from sunset to sunset rather than from midnight to midnight.

Glossary

Brit Chadashah: New covenant, renewed covenant, the New Testament

Gemara: Written commentary on the Oral Law. Part of the Talmud

Meshiach: Messiah, anointed one

Mincha: gift, offering, present, voluntary offering

Mishna: the written collection of the Oral Law. Part of the Talmud

Moed: appointed time or place, appointment, festival. Pl. Moedim

Olah: to ascend or go up, burnt offering

Owth: sign, signal, as an appearing

Talmud: is a record of rabbinic discussions pertaining to Jewish law, ethics, customs, and history. It consists of two parts, the Mishnah and the Gemara.

Tanakh: An acronym for the Hebrew scriptures. The T stands for the Torah which consists of the Books of Moses, the N stands for Navi'im which are the books of the prophets, and the K stands for the Ketuvim which are the writings.

Tallit: cloak, prayer shawl, four cornered garment

Targum: Aramaic translation and interpretation of the Tanakh.

Torah: a precept or statute, especially the Decalogue or Pentateuch, teaching, law.

Yeshua: Given Hebrew name of Jesus. It means he will save.

Additional recommended resources

This is not intended to be an exhaustive list but it is some of the primary research resources that we have used and it will give you a good place to start.

Online resources:

www.biblestudytools.com
    Multiple Bible versions, commentaries and other on-line reference tools.
www.elshaddaiministries.us
    Weekly Torah teachings and other teaching sessions available free on-line.
www.jewishencyclopedia.com

Computer software

Power Bible
    Available at www.powerbible.com
E-Sword
    www.e-sword.net

Printed books or ebooks

Alfred Edersheim:
    The Temple – Its Ministry and Services
    The Bible History: Old Testament
    Sketches of Jewish Social life in the Time of Christ
    The Life and Times of Jesus the Messiah

E. W. Bullinger:
    Numbers in Scripture
    The Witness of the Stars
    Figures of Speech Used in the Bible

Dr. Frank Seekins:
    Hebrew Word Pictures
    The Gospel in Ancient Hebrew
    The Ten Commandments

Strong's Exhaustive Concordance and Dictionary

Made in the USA
Coppell, TX
12 November 2023

24101535R20103